The Index Investing Revolution

How Canadian Investors
Can Make More, Save More
And Worry Less

Brian Noble

MACMILLAN CANADA
TORONTO

Canadian Cataloguing in Publication Data

Noble, D. Brian
    The index investing revolution

Includes index.

ISBN 0-7715-7645-5

1. Index mutual funds 1. Title.

HG4530.N62 1999   332.63'27   C99-931574-9

Cover & interior design: Kyle Gell art and design

1 2 3 4 5   TRANS B-G   03 02 01 00 99

This book is available at special discounts for bulk purchases by your group or organization for sales promotions, premiums, fundraising and seminars. For details, contact: CDG Books Canada, Special Sales Department, 99 Yorkville Avenue, Suite 400, Toronto, ON, M5R 3K5. Tel: 416-963-8830.

Macmillan Canada
An imprint of CDG Books Canada
Toronto

Printed in Canada

Contents

Preface and Acknowledgements

THIS BOOK IS SPECIFICALLY ABOUT INDEX INVESTING, which means employing established index benchmarks as proxies for the various asset classes utilized in the investment management process. In this way, investing is no longer a matter of selecting individual securities or mutual funds for a portfolio, but rather employing asset allocation to create the desired level of exposure to each principal asset class. Asset allocation means apportioning your funds among the major asset classes (basically stocks and fixed-income instruments) in proportion to your investment time horizon, risk tolerance level, specific capital appreciation and income requirements and so on. Readers will certainly find a bias towards the equity component of the asset allocation process here, but that is simply because index investing for most people is about stocks; however, bond indexing will also be discussed at some length. While the principles of index investing have their roots in institutional money management, they can nonetheless be readily and successfully employed by individuals with only small amounts of money to invest. If all of this sounds a mouthful, we'll do our best to explain. But perhaps the best place to start is in the real world.

THE PROFESSOR AND HIS INVESTMENT DILEMMA

Not so long ago, I was invited to a charity luncheon by a client who works at one of the big banks. The group at the bank's table was eclectic, lawyers and PR types, other consultants and one university professor—of modern languages—who happened to be the person I ended up spending the most time talking to. In the grand tradition of Joseph P. Kennedy (one day when he was riding down an elevator in the late 1920s and was being given stock tips by the elevator operator—remember those?—he reportedly realized in a flash that the great American bull market of the flapper age was about to be gored), the general conversation soon turned to personal investing.

Despite the fact that he was tenured and a member of the university pension plan, the professor was concerned about his retirement and had determined to do something about it. He told me that he had recently taken the plunge with $20,000 he felt he could afford to lose. On the advice of his broker, he had bought shares in two major U.S. companies: J.P. Morgan, the venerable investment bank and Dow Jones Industrial Average component, the kind of stock which benefits when the economy is stable or slowing, inflation is muted and interest rates are declining; and Caterpillar, the famous heavy equipment manufacturer and another Dow stock, a so-called "cyclical" that benefits from an overheated economy, rising inflation and higher interest rates.

I conceded that investment exposure to the world's largest, most dynamic economy via its stock market only made sense, but questioned his stock selection. Why, out of a potential universe of about 10,000 stocks currently traded on the major U.S. exchanges, did he choose these two names (Street jargon for stocks) and these two only? What was his rationale for the choice? How well did he think he was going to do? How long did he propose to stay invested? Was he really a trader or an investor? Etc., etc., etc.

I didn't get much of a response to these questions, but presumably the analysis would go something like this:

1. The professor's broker thought that interest rates were going down, so he advised buying an interest-sensitive stock (J.P. Morgan). In

addition, as everybody knows, Morgans is about to start selling bonds over the Internet so its prospects are very bright indeed.

2. The professor's broker thought that interest rates were going up, so he advised buying a cyclical stock (Caterpillar). In addition, as everybody knows, Caterpillar is about to sell heavy construction equipment over the Internet so its prospects are very bright indeed.

3. The professor's broker was either: a) a macro-economic wizard; b) a genius at hedging; c) confused.

4. The professor's broker had also told him that the first principle of investing is establishing at the outset what you are prepared to lose because the odds are that you're going to lose most (or all) of your funds. The idea that portfolio investment can generate a probable (and even positive) return given certain risk/return parameters was presumably alien.

5. The professor bought all of the above arguments when he forked over his $20K.

If the professor thought he was buying exposure to the U.S. economy through its vibrant stock market, he was dreaming. The reality is, he was speculating on two entirely unrelated stocks in two diametrically opposite industries. Would he win or lose? Most likely over time, any gains from the one stock would net out with losses from the other simply because the two stocks in question respond in completely contrasting ways to the same economic and market stimuli. In the mean time, his investment could end up being "dead money" (invested funds that don't go anywhere). He'd probably have been better off leaving his $20K in the bank.

Unfortunately like so many other investors, the professor's approach is hockey-like: he is shooting to score. Equally unfortunately, the odds of "scoring" with individual stocks aren't great. The mentality here is akin to getting psyched up for a day at the track or a trip to Vegas. Next, consider his approach to investing: it's a little like buying a car (the market) by its tires (two stocks). The fact is, stock selection is tricky. With each individual stock, you are taking on equity-specific risk (what if Caterpillar's earnings don't meet Street estimates? What if J.P. Morgan loses big time in the derivative market?) as well as market risk (what if investors don't like stocks any more and buy bonds instead?). What's more, two stocks, no matter how good, don't make a diversified portfolio. Next, modern portfolio theory tells us that asset allocation— not individual security selection—is far and away the most important determinant of investment success. There's a lot more about this subject in Chapter 7. Lastly, the professor is confusing the possibility of absolute gain (i.e. how far his stocks may or may not go up) with comparative gain (i.e. how his stocks will perform vis-à-vis the market as a whole) and assuming considerable risk in betting the farm, particularly if his bet is wrong, which statistically it has a very high probability of being.

There is a better way. For $20,000 (or a lot less), the professor could have bought exposure to the entire U.S. market through units of an index fund or a comparable exchange-traded index product that tracks one of the leading stock market performance benchmarks. If he had real market savvy, he could also consider using index derivatives to manage his portfolio.

Index investing ensures instant portfolio diversification by providing exposure to the entire market through a one-stop investment decision. With index investing, there's no more worrying about which individual stocks to buy or sell and there's no more deciding which sectors to include, exclude, overweight, underweight or whatever. What's more, investment returns are based on the capital appreciation and dividend

stream from a broad spectrum of companies across all major industrial groups. Instead of being dependent on the vicissitudes of one or
two stocks, index investing gives you comprehensive investment exposure to the economy—period. Which is presumably what the professor
was trying to accomplish in the first place. Hence this book.

WHAT WE'RE SELLING AND WHAT WE'RE NOT

If you can relate to the professor's predicament and what must be
the simplest solution to it, read on. This book is not intended to be
technical, but will provide basic answers to your questions about the
how's, why's and benefits of index investing. The recurring Wall Street
to Main Street theme is intended to give individual investors a little
bit of insight into how professional traders use index strategies and
where some index concepts have come from. You won't be offered a
seven figure package on Wall Street after you've finished reading this,
but you should be better informed. There is also no attempt to "sell"
anyone on any particular investment product or supplier, though I will
mention specific products if they are relevant and if they illustrate
the point under discussion. I've tried to be as careful as possible in
checking my facts, but any errors in connection with products mentioned or anything else for that matter are accidental, non-malicious
and basically just reflect incompetence on my part.

I want to be clear on another point: I'm certainly not maintaining
that index investing is the only way to invest. Nor is index investing any
sort of guarantee of not losing money. Rather, it is the idea of index investing that I want to bring into clear view since it can unlock the key
to the concept of asset allocation, which is the essence of rational investing. So if this book is selling anything, it's selling ideas:

- What are indexes all about and how do they work?
- Why should index investing be a core component of your investment strategy?
- Why it is difficult for professional fund managers to consistently beat the index benchmarks.
- What index products are available (equity and fixed income in the U.S., Canada, Europe, Asia and international) and how you can trade them/invest in them.
- What are the benefits of using index products (stocks and bonds primarily but also cash) for effective asset allocation for your portfolio.
- What Wall Street (or Bay Street) can teach Main Street or how to manage your portfolio like a pro using index investing concepts.

One further point of differentiation is the way we're going to look at index investing. We'll be covering not just index funds, but also cash market products such as index participation units and guaranteed index products, and the gamut of index derivatives. Not all of these are appropriate for every investor as they involve different risk profiles and require different forms of investment account. Nonetheless, they have all grown up together and in order to understand the index advantage comprehensively, they must all be given due consideration.

A great deal of this ground has been covered before at length and in depth over many years. In fact, the arguments in favour of index investing haven't changed all that much in almost a generation; it's just that they still haven't really sunk in with the average retail investor. Consider this classic passage from *A Random Walk Down Wall Street*, one of the earliest and most influential "quant" books about investing: "What we need is a no-load, minimum-management-fee mutual fund that simply buys the hundreds of stocks making up the broad stock-market averages and does no trading from security to security in an attempt to catch the winners. Whenever below-average performance on the part of any mutual fund is noticed, fund spokesmen are quick to point out, 'You can't buy the averages.' It's time the public could." By the way, the date is 1973, just a couple of years before the first U.S. index fund (the Vanguard 500 Index Fund) was launched.

As any observant reader will note, there is quite a bit about Vanguard funds throughout this book. I have never had any connection of any sort with Vanguard, but simply have known about their pioneering work in the U.S. index fund business over many years. It is for this reason that it is somewhat embarrassing to admit that I got my hands on Vanguard founder John C. Bogle's latest book, *Common Sense on Mutual Funds* (see further pp. 47 ff.), only when this particular title was about two-thirds completed. *Common Sense* is destined to become an investment classic in the tradition of *The Intelligent Investor, A Random Walk Down Wall Street, The Warren Buffett Way* and so on. If Bogle is the master of index investing, then perhaps this offering may be considered in the tradition of the acolyte Meistersinger.

I want to thank a number of people for their help and assistance. The idea for this book occurred at about 10:30 p.m. on Thursday 17 December 1998 after a very good conversation and dinner at Scaramouche with an old friend, Morgan Eastman of United Capital in Vancouver. Kathy Taylor, CFA of Barclays Global Investors is one of Canada's leading authorities on index investing; she was kind enough to read through the manuscript carefully and critically, sharing her considerable expertise and making extremely pertinent suggestions in the process. Tom Merifield of RBC Dominion Securities has taught me a great deal about derivatives and many other things; I also cajoled him into taking a look at the manuscript to save me from making elementary mistakes. Jonathan Hartman, CFA of Royal Mutual Funds shared his in-depth knowledge of the North American mutual fund industry, for which I am grateful. Andrew Scipio and Richard Austin provided trenchant criticism and many helpful suggestions that have certainly resulted in a better book.

Comrade in arms Gordon Laight, with Best Funds in Nassau and author of the highly acclaimed offshore financial planning and investment book *Offshore Advantage: A Canadian Guide to Wealth Creation, Asset Protection & Estate Planning*, gave me the book writing bug. My old friend from Princeton, New Jersey, John Powers, who founded one of the best investment journals dedicated to index-related and other quantitative asset management issues in the 1980s (called *Intermarket*, now unfortunately long gone), was also a friend to the Canadian index industry (John started his career as a crime reporter. Does that tell you something about the index business?). Paul Ross of Gee Jeffery in Toronto and I have discussed index investing for years and I am as always grateful for his insights and support. Richard Croft of Croft Financial Group and I go back an awfully long way; he and Professor Eric Kirzner of the University of Toronto have been doing some pioneering work in indexing with the *National Post* and remain among the most interesting and informed people to talk to about this subject. My publisher, Robert Harris of CDG Books Canada (parent of Macmillan Canada), has been a tremendous help and staunch ally. While these individuals will, I am sure, agree in large part with what is written here, any errors of fact or judgment are of course entirely mine. Finally, my wife Karen: semper carissima.

CHAPTER I

Investment
Consumerism 101

———

IT'S THE DAY BEFORE a long summer holiday weekend, and you're getting ready to go to the cottage. Naturally, you're also getting ready to play the great Canadian summer pastime: trying to determine who sells the cheapest gas in your neighbourhood. Confronted with prices at two stations, back to back on gasoline alley, which are you going to choose?

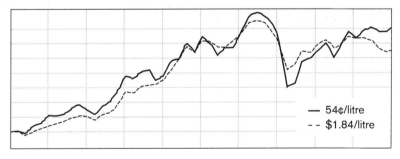

— 54¢/litre
- - $1.84/litre

Performance Comparison

As you can see from the chart, both have the same octane rating at the pump. Both will get you where you want to go. It's just that one costs about 240% more than the other.

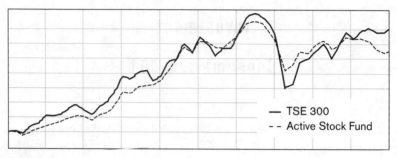

Performance Comparison

In fact, what you have been looking at is the recent performance chart of an actively managed Canadian equity fund versus the TSE 300, still the leading barometer of stock market performance in Canada and incidentally the benchmark against which the active fund manager earns his or her annual bonus.

Surprise, surprise. The active fund, managed by a well-regarded and long-established manager of billions of dollars' worth of pension, mutual fund and other assets, tracks the index uncannily closely. In fact, there are times when you can't tell the difference between the two; and over the longer term, the ups and downs basically net out. So what is the difference? The essential difference is price. The active product costs the investor over 2.25% per year in management and other related fees in addition to the mutual fund load (or commission) paid at the time of acquisition. But exposure to some index products that also track the TSE 300 can be had for as little as 0.05% per year; same basic performance, much, much reduced price.

If Canadian consumers paid the same sort of attention to their investment consumption as they do to gasoline or sundry other mundane articles of everyday life, they'd certainly be much better off. Recent research from *Marketing Solutions*, for example, has shown that something over 60% of Canadian mutual fund consumers did not even realize they were incurring an annual management and expense fee (or MER) for their fund*. In addition, since MERs are effectively hidden (the published return of a mutual fund is net of its MER), they are basically invisible to the average investment consumer.

But this is changing. Many Canadian investors are tired of paying a premium in management fees and loads for mutual funds that chronically fail to outperform the standard index benchmarks. As a result, more and more people are realizing that by investing in index funds and related products that directly track—as opposed to trying to beat—the market they can derive a number of top line benefits:

1. Investors can actually enjoy better returns with index products than actively managed funds because something like 70–80% of active managers fail to outperform the market in any given year. For more on why this is so, and what active managers try to do about it, see pp. 87 ff.
2. Index investing is a one-stop decision that precludes ever having to worry again about what individual stocks to buy. By definition, index investing provides exposure to a well-diversified portfolio that essentially tracks the strength of the economy via the broad market while at the same time smoothing out weakness arising from cyclical, sector or rotational pressures.

---

*The MER comprises the manager's fee (cost of managing the mutual fund) plus all expenses incurred in the management process (e.g. salaries, administrative and marketing expenses, custodial fees, etc., but not transaction costs, i.e. brokerage commissions) expressed as a percentage of the fund's net assets. It is the handiest measure of what it costs to own a fund.

3. Index fund investors typically pay no loads and much less in annual management and related fees than consumers of actively managed fund products. Canadian index fund MERs typically range from 0.90% on the high side to 0.50% on the low side versus 2.25–2.50% for actively managed funds; and much less again for exchange-traded index products. In the U.S., the story is even better.

4. In terms of executing their own individual strategies, index investing enables investors to focus on the big picture. This is called asset allocation, and we'll talk about the concept of asset allocation throughout this book and in detail in Chapter 7.

5. Index products tend to exhibit less volatility than many active funds because they provide the pure index return, not diluted by any cash position (see Chapter 4). This return is "guaranteed" to the extent that index funds ensure you will match if not exceed overall market or more specifically index performance. As the stock market return has averaged in excess of 10% per year over a very long time horizon, such "matching" isn't such a bad prospect at all.

This logic has not escaped sophisticated institutional investors and the trend towards index investing is growing rapidly in both Canada and the U.S. Consider these facts which a give a sense of the order of magnitude of the impetus towards the index investing revolution:

- Index investing is big business in the U.S. and globally. Total assets committed to index management are conservatively estimated to be in the range of US$2 *trillion*—that's about four times the size of the entire Canadian economy. This is largely big pension, mutual fund and other institutional money. For example, the state employee pension plan of California (CALPERS) is a major in-dexer with billions committed to index (so-called "passive" man-agement) programs. The second biggest mutual fund in the U.S. and indeed the world is an equity index fund.

- In Canada today, about $35 billion in pension fund assets (out of a total universe of approximately $520 billion) are invested in index-related strategies (this number has about tripled since 1993).
- At year-end 1998, the universe of retail index assets in Canada were estimated at around $8 billion (up from $700 million in 1990).
- Canadian banks report that about 40% of their total equity mu-tual fund assets are now index products. In fact, the big banks have been in the vanguard of promoting index investing in this country. We'll explore how they used indexing to translate mar-ket (i.e. their market share) adversity into opportunity later.
- The new S&P/TSE 60 Index was launched in Canada at the be-ginning of 1999. This index has been acclaimed as the new stan-dard for the Canadian stock market and will create renewed excitement about index investing in Canada. It also looks as if cash market and derivative product development will follow soon. This should be good news for all Canadian investors.

Put it all together and you'll see that indexing is part of a trend that is revolutionizing the way money is managed not just in North America but also around the world. While investors generally aren't revolutionary, they are also not reactionary. So if you see the logic of this trend, let's proceed to consider what indexes are all about, who uses them and how they can be part of your overall financial plan.

To repeat, the bottom line is that indexing is a one-stop investment decision that provides the basis for effective, personal asset allocation.

What's more, since academic research indicates that 90% of investment performance is all about asset allocation, why would anyone still be picking stocks? Then there's the cost angle: why pay more for "performance" (i.e. active management) when you know it doesn't work 70–80% of the time? Some recent if selective history underlines the wisdom of giving careful thought to these questions.

1998–MOMENT OF TRUTH FOR INDEX INVESTING?

Fidelity's recent ad blitz in the U.S. financial media underscores the fundamental decision that all equity investors must make: "How was it possible to beat the S&P 500 Index in 1998? Just ask some of the Fidelity fund managers who did." Fine and true; something like half a dozen Fidelity funds did beat the broadly based S&P 500 Index (about which we will have a great deal to say starting with Chapter 2), and given the fact that the S&P 500 was up 28.7%, that is indeed an accomplishment. But consider the facts regarding the performance of the two leading U.S. equity funds in 1998 and then make up your own mind. If you want to find out more about U.S. fund performance in general, consult Morningstar (www.morningstar.net), a very useful resource for any investor.

The gargantuan $84 billion Fidelity Magellan Fund (the biggest mutual fund in the U.S. and indeed the world; assets quoted as at year-end 1998) returned 29.6% last year with an average risk factor*. The $70 billion Vanguard 500 Index Fund (which tracks the S&P 500

---

*There are different ways to measure portfolio risk. Here's a nifty one called the Sharpe ratio after the Nobel-winning economist. The Sharpe ratio calculates the difference between the return on an investment and the return on a risk-free investment (usually T-bills) and divides it by the investment's standard deviation, the most common measure of volatility or risk. The ratio tells you how much excess return the investment has delivered per unit of risk.

Index and is the second biggest in the U.S., but certainly much less well known to Canadian investors) returned 28.6% with a low risk factor*. Magellan (which is currently closed to new investors) costs 0.61% in annual management fees plus a 3% load; by comparison the Vanguard 500 fund costs just 0.18% and is no load. By Canadian standards, these MERs are shockingly low (the average expense ratio for all U.S. equity funds is about 1.5% and for the large funds tracked by Morningstar about 1.3%), but that's another story. In addition, the Vanguard 500 fund outperformed all but 12% of actively managed U.S. equity funds in 1998. Incidentally, the average U.S. stock fund had a hard time delivering a 10% return last year. Looking at the cost/benefit comparison between the two U.S. fund behemoths in tabular form may make it easier:

	% Return	MER	Cost Factor
Magellan	29.6%	0.61%	3.4X more expensive
Vanguard 500	28.6%	0.18%	

Now let's look closer to home. While the Canadian stock market as measured by the TSE 300 Composite Index has been a dismal performer in recent years, the performance of active versus index investors in 1998 nonetheless confirmed the U.S. experience. Instead of using an index mutual fund, the index proxy this time will be TIPS 35 (see Chapter 3 for more about TIPS), a cash market product comprised of the largest capitalization stocks that trade on the Toronto Stock Exchange; the S&P 500 Index equivalent is called SPDRs (again, see Chapter 3).

1998 was another down year for the Canadian market: TIPS were off 0.07%, but the average large-cap Canadian stock fund showed a negative 2.9% return. Leaving aside the question of mutual fund loads or brokerage commissions for index participation units, the average annual management/expense fee or MER for a domestic equity fund is around 2.25% (no name calling is desired so a generic example will do); TIPS charge just 0.05%. That translates into a better (even if negative) return at a lot less cost. Again, a short table punches home the point:

% Return	MER	Cost Factor	
Active fund X	-2.9%	2.25%	45X more expensive
TIPS 35	-0.07%	0.05%	

If we put on our investment consumer hats for a moment, cost/benefit analysis demands just two things: what are we getting and what are we paying for it? For avid comparative shoppers, further comment should be superfluous. It should also be clear, particularly from the U.S. example, that when choosing between funds posting returns within such a comparatively narrow range and holding so many stocks in common (as they do), you may as well pick the one that's cheapest to own. So the basic question for investment consumers to consider is this: is marginally better performance (or worse performance in the case of the Canadian example) worth the extra fees and potentially greater portfolio risk? It is also worth remembering that actively managed funds (such as Magellan, which has outperformed as well as underperformed throughout its existence) may or may not beat the index bogey in any given year. By definition, indexes are the market and index fund performance is "guaranteed" to the extent that it will mirror the market return minus some slippage due to the MER, transaction costs and other technical factors.

The experience of one year in the market doesn't make for a successful retirement nest egg and so on and so on and so on. But the first point about the index advantage has been made.

Index Advantage # 1: Investment performance comes at a cost. If you can pay less for comparable performance, why would you not consider doing so?

THAT WAS THEN—THIS IS NOW

The 1980s and early 90s were the era of the macho fund manager, trader and professional investor. Remember Michael Douglas as Gordon Gekko in *Wall Street?* Remember Ivan Boesky, the model for greed is good? Remember October 19, 1987?

In the 1980s, life imitated art and vice versa. Peter Lynch, the former Fidelity superstar who placed Magellan at the top of the charts, became and still is almost a cult figure, appearing with other celebrities on television ads and so on. Unfortunately for Magellan investors, his successor made a massively wrong bet on the bond market (excuse me, this was supposed to be a stock fund, wasn't it? See *Games Managers Play*, Chapter 4), tarnishing his reputation as well as Fidelity's. As we have seen, the current Magellan manager has turned things around for the world's biggest mutual fund, but very few people outside the business today could tell you his name.

In Canada, we had Frank Mersch, the ex-Altamira manager who handily beat the TSE in a recessionary, down market environment for several years by making gigantic bets and dominating trading in a number of junior resource stocks; he subsequently left the industry under a cloud. I remember attending an Altamira public seminar (it was paid attendance; I was consulting for them at the time), which felt more like a southern Baptist revival meeting than any sort of investor symposium I've ever been at. Trimark's patient value focus, team approach and savvy in selling to the dealer community has garnered positive press along with impressive numbers since the mid-1980s; they have stumbled badly, however, in the recent growth environment as well as experiencing considerable manager turnover. Dynamic's portfolio focus was resource stocks and very short-term bonds, both of which proved to be disastrous calls and resulted in the departure of two respected managers. Prominent growth manager Wayne Deans of the eponymous Deans Knight in Vancouver has seen his star tarnished and has lost sub-advisory business as a result of poor performance. Even Alex Christ, one of the deans of Canadian professional investors, saw his performance track record at Mackenzie badly eroded through a misreading of the macro-economic environment. More cynically, Mackenzie proved once and for all that investment products are sold, not bought.

There are global legends like Warren Buffett and Sir John Templeton, who have been appropriately lionized as Heldeninvestors despite the occasional bad year. But what about other U.S. and international superstars? Mark Mobius, the emerging markets guru at Franklin Templeton, is still in media view but the Templeton bargain basement investment style suffered badly from the Asian crisis in 1997–1998 and the market panic in the fall of 1998. Ken Heebner, whose conversational duelling ads you have probably noticed on CNBC, has seen his previously strong performance steadily eroded, and his longer-term rates of return as presented on the tube have mysteriously started to shrink. The previously high-flying Mutual Series, established by legendary value investor Michael Price, saw nearly all its funds in the bottom half of their respective categories in 1998. The list goes on and on.

What god, man, or hero
Shall I place a tin wreath upon!—*Ezra Pound*

If investing in the 1980s was all about heroics and hero worship, today the emphasis seems to be more on self-reliance and figuring it out for yourself. Ten years ago, many individual investors didn't know how to interpret a price earnings (P/E) multiple or understand what book value means; consequently, they turned their money over to fund managers who presumably did. The simple expectation of most investors was that their manager would do a better job of picking stocks than they could. But now with the advent of Internet day trading, online advisory services, chat rooms and the rest of it, the growing ranks of do-it-yourself investors not only think that they can do a better job than professional managers—they know they can. What's even more heterodoxical, more and more people (as well as the front covers of prominent financial and investment publications) are asking the unthinkable: do investors need fund managers at all?

The problem goes beyond the fact that comparatively few active managers are able to match/beat the indexes consistently or conversely that passively managed funds have outperformed all but a few actively managed funds over the last few years. In the U.S., the popularity of indexing and the public's perception that active managers simply can't outperform show that many investors no longer believe that active mutual funds are a viable option any more. Cash inflows of something like $25 billion into U.S. index funds in 1998 attest to that.

It must be said, however, that U.S. market performance over the past few years has been exceptional and highly focused. In the inclusive four year period from 1995–98, the S&P 500 has posted average annual returns of just over 30%. The S&P 500 in turn comprises a select group of large-cap growth stocks heavily represented by the financial services, technology, healthcare and consumer sectors which have clearly been the place to be during this period. The S&P 500 also hasn't been cheap. Many fund managers have been reared in a value-oriented investment management discipline. Investing in large-cap growth stocks trading at historically high valuations (usually expressed by their P/E multiples) has really been counterintuitive to a great number of active managers. Index watchers have also pointed out that while the S&P 500 outperformed the market (i.e. the other major equity indexes) in 1998, the top 30-50 stocks that make up the lion's share of the S&P 500 market cap actually outperformed the index itself. Because their huge market caps give them a disproportionate weighting in the overall index, the Nifty 50 as they have been termed have a disproportionate effect on its overall return (see Chapter 2). In fact, if you had invested in the bottom 250 stocks that make up the S&P 500, you would have actually lost money in 1998.

All true and good. Investment success with an index fund ultimately derives from the success of all the companies that comprise the index itself. There is no mystery here. But unless you choose to believe that a well-designed, highly diversified index does not represent a good proxy for the broader stock market and in turn for the economy as a whole, then indexing is a form of insurance against over- and/or underexposure to potentially under- and/or overperforming sectors of the market. The beauty of index investing is that it does provide instant diversification such that, if the bottom-tier stocks outperform and the top-tier stocks underperform or vice versa, you have a proportionate degree of investment exposure nonetheless.

Investors can't have it both ways. The index does indeed produce an "average" return, but a 13.5% annual "average return" from 1973–98 in the case of the S&P 500 is nothing to be sneezed at.

Index Advantage # 2: What sectors of the market will outperform or underperform in any given year is basically unpredictable. If you can at least ensure that you have exposure to all sectors of the market, why would you not consider doing so?

NOBODY SAID THERE'S A FREE LUNCH

Up until now, there has been a heavy U.S. focus in our discussion about index investing. That is because, as in so many other things, the U.S. market has led the way. It is also undeniable that we've had problems with our indexes in Canada (does anyone really use the Montreal market index?). In addition, a number of fund families, including the AIC group and other sector funds, have massively outperformed the TSE 300 over long time horizons. But that is changing and the structural problems of Canadian indexes are being addressed (see Chapter 2). Consequently, Canadian investors could do well to give consideration to index principles rather than spend their time praying for another domestic equivalent of Peter Lynch to come along.

We've already considered some of the major benefits of index investing. But there are others, largely more technical:

1. Investors would generally have difficulty being able to afford to buy all 30, 35, 300 or 500 stocks that comprise a major index. With an index fund or equivalent, you can own a highly diversified portfolio consisting of all these stocks in one trade, with one transaction cost, even with only a small amount of money.

2. With index products, portfolio—and portfolio manager—turnover is kept to a minimum. That means fund transaction costs (brokerage fees for buying and selling stock, etc.) are low (don't forget you are paying for transaction costs every time your fund buys or sells a stock). Also remember how you felt the day you read in the paper that your hot fund manager had just left your fund company—and presumably had just left you holding the bag? There are positive tax implications here as well

since heavy trading triggers taxable capital gains which are passed on directly to unitholders; index funds are not heavy traders.

3. In chasing hot stocks, with their promise of instant riches, you're going to suffer from a variety of factors that imperil any sort of sensible pricing. Similarly, liquidity or the ability to get at your money when you need it can be nightmare, particularly in the lower-tier stocks of an index such as the TSE 300. With an index product, however, you get exposure to a diversified portfolio of stocks without having to worry that you've paid up for an individual stock on the way in and are getting taken on the way out. You've simply bought the market lock, stock and barrel.

4. Index products also provide regular cash flow from dividends. The dividend yield is very important to portfolio returns over time, but too many individual investors focus exclusively on capital growth, not total return (the combination of the two). Again, there is no mystery here: reinvested dividends augment returns over the long term through simple compounding.

5. Some types of index product (exchange-traded index units and derivatives, but not mutual funds) enable you to short-sell the market in order to let you profit in the event of a price decline. This is a strategy usually only appropriate for deep-pocketed traders, but short-selling to hedge an existing portfolio can also provide a measure of insurance against market volatility (more on this in Chapter 8).

The most significant advantage of index investing, however, remains cost/benefit. We have observed the phenomenon of active manager underperformance. The numbers vary, but in any given year, something like 70–80% of active managers in the U.S. fail to beat their index benchmark (the number is lower in Canada but still significant, around 50–60%). Why this is so is a result of a combination of factors. Corporate earnings estimates, which are the locomotive propelling stock valuations, are notoriously volatile; it has been said that the volatility of analysts' earnings estimates is far greater than the volatility of the underlying stocks they cover. In other words, analysts get earnings wrong big time, too much of the time. Next, a manager's style can be out of sync with the market (for instance, the bargain basement value style is at variance with the current growth/momentum market that we've been experiencing). Then there is portfolio size or the problem of managing strong asset growth. Large portfolios soon tend to look like index funds (a phenomenon known as "closet indexing," see Chapter 4) because managers are constrained by liquidity considerations from taking positions in potentially outperforming second and third tier stocks; put another way, even a star-performing small-cap stock can't make much of a contribution to performance in a billion dollar portfolio.

For these and other reasons, the active manager's job is indeed a difficult one. In the world of pension fund investing, Canadian equity managers are generally expected to outperform the index by 2–3 percentage points (a feat that few are able to achieve). Given that MERs for Canadian equity mutual funds are generally in the 2–2.5% range, the likelihood of mutual funds achieving above-market performance that eludes institutional funds is slim to say the least. So even before the manager gets to the office in the morning, he/she is hobbled by one major impediment to performance: the fund MER. When a fund is charging 2.5% right off the top, the manager is already running behind in terms of making money for the portfolio even before the annual performance clock starts ticking. When the market is rip-roaring away, such levels of management and expense fees aren't particularly worrying to many investors, but if we move into an era of lessened performance expectations, they will start to stick out like a sore thumb. This structural cost problem is really at the heart of the argument in favour of index investing.

The other overwhelming problem with active management is that there is no such thing as 20/20 foresight. It is quite simply impossible to infer from past returns what future performance is likely to be. So regardless of absolute performance, a dollar invested in the average active fund net of costs will always underperform the average dollar invested in an index fund simply because active funds have a much higher fee structure. In other words, while capital growth or fund performance is hard or indeed impossible to predict, costs are very easy to predict. This is precisely the sort of consumer 101 logic that informs the way large modern pension funds and other institutional investors in the U.S. and Canada are managing their assets today. Thanks to the index investing revolution, now you can, too.

Index Advantage # 3: Investment performance is basically unpredictable. If you can pay less for comparable performance, why would you not consider doing so?

CHAPTER 2

A Short History
of Indexes

———

THE WORD "INDEX" LITERALLY means forefinger—that is, something that points out what is happening or points the way. Increasingly, the index investing revolution has been pointing the way for North American investors as they search for efficient and cost-effective ways to create financial security for themselves and their families.

We are used to various forms of "index" from barometers, thermometers and speedometers to the federal government's unemployment index or Consumer Price Index (CPI), but investment indexes (or indices if you prefer the Latinate form) are essentially a late 19th century creation. In 1896, Charles Dow introduced his now-famous stock "average" or index so that investors could have a convenient way of following the New York equity market. At the end of each trading day, Dow would calculate the average price of 12 stocks and publish it in an investor newsletter which has now become *The Wall Street Journal*. Today, the Dow Jones Industrial Average (DJIA or Dow) comprises 30 of the best-known companies in the world, including major industrials (such as AT&T, Boeing, Caterpillar, DuPont, General Electric, General Motors, etc.), food giants (Coke, McDonalds), consumer product manufacturers and retailers (Procter & Gamble, Eastman Kodak, Sears, Wal-Mart), financial powerhouses (American Express, Citigroup and the professor's choice, J.P. Morgan), and many other household names, including Hewlett Packard, IBM, Walt Disney and so on.

Where Dow led, others have followed and today there are several other U.S. indexes every bit as or even more important than the Dow. The S&P 500 Index comprises 500 of the most important companies in America, including all of the 30 Dow names, and is widely followed in the institutional investment community, while the Wilshire 5000 contains virtually all actively traded stocks in the U.S. The NYSE Composite Index tracks about 2,900 stocks traded on the New York Stock Exchange, whereas the Nasdaq Composite is usually associated with the high-growth technology companies that trade on what has become the new combined Nasdaq/Amex site (the old curb market and poor sister to the other exchanges, the American Stock Exchange merged with the Nasdaq early in 1999).

In Canada, the Toronto 300 Composite Index (TSE 300) was launched January 1, 1977 and will presumably die at some point in the future despite the cheeriness of the Exchange and S&P on this point (more on this to come). The Toronto 35 Index, launched a decade later, was an attempt to create a tradable index that would provide the springboard for a liquid cash market/derivatives tripod (see below). A new Toronto index, the S&P/TSE 60, started being calculated in effect at the beginning of 1999 and will most likely become the primary Canadian equity benchmark and the basis for new index investment product development in future.

Indexes are created to fulfil specific measurement functions. The Dow, S&P 500, Nasdaq 100 and Toronto 35 measure the performance of the very largest companies usually, but not always, by their market capitalization (float or outstanding number of shares times share price). Other indexes focus on mid-size companies (the S&P MidCap 400 or Russell 3000), small companies (the Russell 2000 and S&P SmallCap 600), international companies (Morgan Stanley Capital International Europe, Australasia and Far East (EAFE) Index sponsored by the U.S. investment powerhouse) and even bonds (Lehman Brothers Aggregate Bond Index in the U.S. and ScotiaMcLeod Universe Bond Index or SMU in Canada). Bond indexing is a rather new concept and we'll have more to say about it in Chapter 6.

As we have seen, active managers have had a hard time beating the major big-cap indexes such as the S&P 500 over the last few years, but in general smaller cap indexes and many international indexes have not outperformed a majority of actively managed funds in their peer group. This may change, however, in future as the small-cap and international markets become more efficient. It is also worth noting that the stocks in the big-cap indexes offer enormous liquidity which has in no small measure made them the equities of choice for North American institutional investors. The concept of liquidity (which basically means ease of trading, particularly in size) is going to crop up again and again, so let's take a moment to define it better. In simple terms, if you have 10,000 shares of Royal Bank (large-cap stock of a major financial institution) to sell and somebody else has 10,000 shares of Strategic Value (small-cap stock of a small independent mutual fund company) to sell, who do you think is going to have the easier time getting a fill?

But liquidity means more than that. Liquidity is the ability to turn a dollar into something else that can yield a higher return than the dollar can on its own, and then readily be able to convert that something else back into a dollar when you want to, when you need to. The dollar (or cash, usually represented by T-bills in portfolio management) is the "riskless" asset because you know you'll always get it back in one piece and you know precisely what it is going to earn you—which is generally not very much. With bonds, you can be sure of your yield, but not your principal until the bond matures, which makes bonds like cash from a yield perspective but also riskier than cash because of uncertainty about capital values while you hold the securities. With stocks, the truly "risky" asset, you never know exactly what you're going to get back at the end of the day, but historically you can anticipate a higher return than with the other two. Liquidity or the comparative ease of getting in and out of risky assets is a great solace and enables you to want to take risk in the first place.

In addition to a short history of the development of the key indexes, emphasis will also be placed on their use as performance benchmarks in the investment industry because this is one key to understanding the logic of index investing, i.e. how investment professionals get paid. Please see page 38 for a laundry list of the other indexes of interest to most investors. Index construction is also important because the major indexes are calculated quite differently (e.g. the Dow is a price-weighted index; the S&P 500 is market capitalization weighted; the TSE 300 is a modified market cap index, etc. See below). Individual investors should not, however, overly concern themselves with the minutiae of index construction since the indexes themselves are a given; nobody except the professors makes any money spending time on this kind of thing. In any case, the exchanges put out all sorts of statistical data and other material on how they construct/modify/ update, etc. their indexes which can be accessed online. For a Canadian investor, the dominance of U.S. indexes and the comparative failure of Canadian indexes is also significant, although the outlook for the new S&P/TSE 60 and anticipated family of derivative and cash market vehicles should be positive.

One last consideration. Some extremely sophisticated commentators have made observations that seem to question the validity of indexes per se. For example, Nuala Beck of New Economy fame has identified the TSE 300 as "old economy." The same could be also said of many Dow and S&P 500 component stocks. The mathematician Ron Dembo in his recent book *Seeing Tomorrow* makes this interesting statement: "An entire industry has grown up to track fund managers against indices and one another. Few pension funds have questioned whether these benchmarks make sense. Often, because funds have unique asset-liability profiles, they need highly idiosyncratic benchmarks…yet (they) probably hire managers whose stated goal is to outperform the S&P 500 index." The latter is philosophically a hard one, though I could not presume to comment on the mathematical/risk management reasoning behind it. But either you accept conventional benchmarks or you do not. In *Accepting the Universe*, the author quotes Carlyle on the occasion of his being informed that a very grand lady had come to the realization that she accepted the universe. He replied succinctly, "By God, sir, she'd better."

THE DOW JONES INDUSTRIAL AVERAGE

If not the world's oldest or even first stock market index, the Dow Jones Industrial Average (DJIA or Dow) is unquestionably its most famous. When Dow 10,000 was broached in April 1999, the financial press gasped and CNBC conducted a multi-hour market extravaganza celebrating the event. Curiously, much of the conversation was very much in the logical positivist tradition of Russell and Ayer, focusing on whether

Dow 10,000 had any meaning or not. While the media scrum can only reinforce the notion that where the Dow goes, the public will follow, its fame is really out of all proportion to its use as a benchmark or vehicle for index investors.

Nonetheless, the Dow is the world's most widely followed stock market indicator, tracking just 30 stocks out of a universe of almost 3,000 traded on the New York Stock Exchange (NYSE), again the world's largest exchange (it briefly lost its primacy to Tokyo in the late 1980s). The Dow is computed and the index (technically the Dow is an average, but for our purposes the terms index and average will be interchangeable) transmitted in real time continuously throughout the trading day around the world; responsibility for maintaining and updating the index rests with the editors of *The Wall Street Journal*. Note that the Dow Jones Company, and not the NYSE, is responsible for its construction and the inclusion/deletion of companies in/from the index.

In the 1880s and 90s, the original publishers Messrs. Dow and Jones produced handwritten daily newsletters called "flimsies" which were delivered by messenger to subscribers in the Wall Street area. As their publishing venture flourished—and the newsletter business evolved into a full-blown newspaper—the first Dow Jones average, effectively a transportation index composed of railroad stocks, appeared in 1884. Introduction of the 12-stock industrial average followed in 1896. At first, the average was published irregularly, but daily publication began in *The Wall Street Journal* on October 7, 1896. In 1916, the industrial average was expanded to include 20 stocks; in 1928, it was increased to 30, where it remains today. Of the original 12 Dow stocks, only one, General Electric, is still in the index. Several companies included in the 1896 group are ancestors of firms that are currently very much in business. In terms of big hitters, GM joined the Dow in 1915; Sears Roebuck 1924; IBM in 1979; and Walt Disney in 1991.

Today, the 30 Dow stocks are those of some of the most important companies in the world and are widely held by individual and institutional investors. In terms of market valuation, the Dow currently represents about 20% of the approximately $9 trillion market value of all U.S. stocks and 25% of the value of all stocks listed on the Big Board as the New York Stock Exchange is also known. The Dow is further broken down into sector sub-indexes, including chemicals, Internet, health care, real estate, financial services, petroleum, technology, transports and utilities.

With no computer or even pocket calculator to assist him, Dow had to tote up the closing prices of each index component stock daily and divide that number by a divisor, i.e. the total number of stocks. This produces a price-weighted average, which is one reason why the Dow is still called an average, not an index. Because it is price weighted (as opposed to market capitalization weighted as is the case with the S&P 500), the stocks with the highest prices have the greatest effect on the performance of the index. Just think about that for a moment. The Dow gives more weight to a high-priced stock (an IBM) rather than a lower-priced one (such as an Alcoa). Generally speaking, the price of a stock per se is irrelevant except insofar as it relates to its earnings (stocks are valued on the basis of P/E multiples, which reflect how many times current earnings the stock is trading at). A $100 stock is not necessarily worth more than a $10 stock; it simply has a higher price. But the Dow fails to make this distinction. In an attempt to compensate for the relative lack of sophistication of its computation method, in 1928 the editors of *The Wall Street Journal* began calculating the average with a special divisor to avoid distortions when index companies split their shares or when one stock was substituted for another. Aside from this, nothing has changed since.

When the Dow was first launched, Wall Street was a far different place from what it is today. That's because in the 19th and well into the 20th century, stocks were truly a gamble and gentlemen preferred bonds. As late as Ben Graham in the 1940s and 50s, a rational academic case had to be made for investing in equities as opposed to bonds, which after all promise a return of capital as well as a return on capital. In essence, the 19th century stock market was the wild west, populated by great speculators, blind pool operators, raiders, legendary short-sellers and bears: Livermore, Harriman and Gould to name a few. Price fixing was a given. "Water" was not something you drank, it was what was in stocks. Despite the fact that his office was just across the street, J.P. Morgan Senior (a gentleman whose business was bonds) is reputed never to have set foot inside the NYSE, though he helped avert and/or manage several stock market panics.

Today, with individuals holding billions of dollars worth of mutual funds and institutional and pension fund managers managing trillions, there is more stock market participation in North America than at any other time in history, and stocks are routinely considered safe invest-ment vehicles, even by conservative investors. The Dow played a major role in bringing about this revolution by providing visibility (trans-parency in the jargon of the regulators) to what the stock market is doing as well as a convenient price discovery mechanism (what will the market do today?) that everybody can relate to.

The Dow has also been amenable to changing with the times, though given the explosive growth and rivalry from the tech-laden Nasdaq, some professionals think that it may have lost considerable sway. Nonetheless, the New Economy came to the Dow in 1997, when Hewlett-Packard, Johnson & Johnson, Travelers Group and Wal-Mart replaced Bethlehem Steel, Texaco, Westinghouse and Woolworth in the index. This was the largest change in the composition of the Dow in recent history, and except for the Travelers merger with Citicorp to form Citigroup in 1998, the Dow has not changed since.

Despite criticisms that it represents only a narrow group of 30 industrial companies and that its index calculation is so primitive that no other leading index has followed its lead, the Dow remains what Jim and Jean Q. Investor use to measure the market each and every day. Regardless of its inadequacies, the Dow is quite simply something that everyone understands and can accept.

Dow Jones Transportation Average

While the Dow Jones Industrial Average is the best-known U.S. stock index, it is not the oldest. As we have seen, the Dow Jones Transportation Average has that distinction. The railroads played a pivotal role in the 19th century U.S. economy just as they were the agents of nationhood and growth in Canada. The first Dow Jones index was composed of nine railroads, including the New York Central and Union Pacific, and two non-rails, Pacific Mail Steamship and Western Union. Over the years, the railroads were joined by other transportation companies such as Delta, Fedex and Ryder. In keeping with the times, the railroad average was renamed the transportation average (called the "trannies" on the Street) in 1970 and now has 20 constituent stocks.

This index is very important to market technicians (analysts who chart market and individual stock performance). According to Dow theory (not directly connected with the original Charles Dow), the Dow Jones Transportation Average must "confirm" the direction of the Dow industrials on the upside and the downside for a market trend to have validity. For instance, if the industrials reach a new high, the transports must also new high to confirm the trend. The original thinking here was that, if the economy is strong and the industrials are profiting, then it would be peculiar if the transportation sector was not (i.e. you have to get the goods to market somehow—or as go the rails, so goes the economy). Even today, you still hear about Dow theory and whether or not the transports have confirmed. It only stands to reason, however, that in the Internet age (though it is true that a company like Fedex ships what e-commerce sells), the adherents of Dow theory should become fewer and fewer.

Dow Jones Utility Average

The Dow Jones Utility Average ("utes" in Street talk) is the most recent of the three Dow Jones averages, having made its debut in 1929, a pretty auspicious year in market history. The utility average is comprised of 15 large U.S. electricity and natural gas companies and also serves as a proxy for interest rates in addition to tracking the major utilities. On the basis of the normal inverse relationship between bond prices and interest rates (when bond prices rise, rates fall and vice versa), a rise in the utility index indicates falling interest rates, while a decline is a function of rising interest rates. Because of its interest-rate sensitivity, the utility average is also regarded by many analysts as a leading indicator for the stock market as a whole.

THE S&P 500 INDEX

While the Dow is the more popular stock index, the S&P 500 is the most widely used, especially by professional investors. This broadly based index is also much more representative of the market and rests on a better foundation (market cap weighting) than the Dow; in any event, it's against the S&P 500 that the bonus cheques are most frequently cut on Wall Street. Like the Dow, the S&P complex of indexes is ultimately owned by the major publishing concern McGraw-Hill.

Standard & Poor's (the large rating agency, financial data management company and McGraw-Hill subsidiary) developed the first market capitalization weighted index in 1926, the much smaller S&P 90. By the late 1950s, this index had evolved into the S&P 500, the benchmark most widely used by professional money managers today. It is instructive to remember, however, that the S&P 500 was never intended to be any sort of investment product or the basis for (index) investment products.

Then as now, the 500 stocks in the S&P 500 are chosen by Standard and Poor's based on a series of criteria, predominantly representation by industry sector, liquidity (ready ability to trade the stock) and stability (both financial and qualitative standards apply). It is important to note that the stocks in the S&P 500 are not necessarily (though they usually are) the 500 largest companies in the U.S., but are chosen to reflect the diversity of the U.S. economy as represented by its stock market. In effect, they are the who's who of corporate America. The S&P 500 is further broken down into sub-indexes, including the S&P 100 index (ticker symbol: OEX), which measures very large company market performance and is the basis for the most successful index options contract ever devised (same ticker), and the S&P 400, the leading U.S. mid-cap index.

The S&P 500 Index is calculated using a "base-weighted aggregate" methodology, which means that the level of the index reflects the total market value of all 500 component stocks relative to a particular base period. The total market value of the index is determined by multiplying the price of each component stock by the number of its shares outstanding. Total returns are calculated by adding quarterly dividend income plus price appreciation for any given time period. What all this means is that the largest stocks (by market cap, not price per se; compare this to the way the Dow works) account for the largest percentage of the index. For example, Microsoft (a Nasdaq and S&P 500 stock, but not a Dow component), which surpassed $500 billion in market cap this year and is the largest company in the U.S., represents about 4% of the S&P 500. Consequently, an S&P 500 index fund would have to have about 4% of its assets invested in Miscosoft in order to capture the index return.

Like all other S&P indexes, the S&P 500 always contains the number of stocks indicated by its name (i.e. 500). Standard & Poor's is responsible for the overall management of the index and takes into account each prospective company's market value, industry group, market capitalization, trading activity, financial health and operating condition before making a decision to list the stock. New companies are added only when there is a vacancy in the index; this is a very exclusive club and there is no desire to expand it. Companies are removed from the S&P 500 as a result of merger or acquisition activity, financial or operating failure, corporate restructuring and so on. Nobody goes willingly.

The history of the S&P isn't as romantic as the Dow, but it's the index to watch in terms of market performance and it's the index that so much index product has been designed around. Since getting into the S&P 500 is big business for American business, stock prices can tend to zoom in expectation of this event (see *Pop Goes the Index*, Chapter 4).

THE NASDAQ COMPOSITE INDEX

The NASD (National Association of Securities Dealers) is the umbrella regulatory body and market sponsor for the U.S. over-the-counter or OTC market. The Nasdaq (National Association of Securities Dealers Automated Quotations System) launched its first index in 1971. Unlike the NYSE or TSE, the Nasdaq has no formal exchange floor or market makers; instead, it is a purely electronic market matching buyers and sellers via the telephone, private wire and computers through a vast U.S.

and global network of brokers and dealers. Established as a non-profit association of brokers and dealers in 1939, the NASD is a self-regulating organization (SRO), just like the TSE or NYSE, which means it has responsibility for ensuring market integrity through various market compliance and surveillance procedures. The Nasdaq merged with the third U.S. exchange, the Amex, to form the Nasdaq-Amex Marketsite in 1999.

Traditionally, shares of junior and/or relatively new companies were traded in the OTC market and the Nasdaq was generally associated with smaller cap equities. With the advent of high-tech companies, and their preference for raising equity rather than debt (as was the case with the Microsoft, Intel, Oracle, etc. and so many of the other tech initial public offerings of securities or IPOs), the Nasdaq has really come into its own. This latter point is interesting because in the period after the collapse of the Milken-inspired junk bond market of the 1980s and early 90s, many high-tech companies had little recourse to capital other than selling themselves (i.e. their equity), not their ability to repay principal and (very high) interest. The Nasdaq has clearly been a major beneficiary of this trend.

The Nasdaq is the third largest market in the world, after the New York and Tokyo exchanges, and handles about 50% of all shares traded by the major U.S. markets. More than 5,300 U.S. and global companies have their stocks traded on the Nasdaq. While the Nasdaq Composite tracks the broader market, the Nasdaq 100 Index was introduced in 1985 to represent the 100 largest stocks by market capitalization and the most active non-financial domestic and international issues listed on the Nasdaq. While high-tech and other innovative companies have typically flocked to the Nasdaq, some have subsequently migrated to the Big Board.

Markets are made as NASD members trade securities with each other at wholesale prices while selling retail to non-members. This has given rise to complaints about bad pricing (primarily overly large bid/ask spreads for many securities) and a subsequent SEC-imposed fine on member firms several years ago. Nonetheless, much wealth has been created by Nasdaq stocks during this decade. Approximately 150 Canadian companies are also interlisted on the Nasdaq/Amex Marketsite.

Originally based on market capitalization like the S&P 500, the Nasdaq 100 Index was changed to a modified market capitalization weighted index (like the TSE 300) late in 1998. This is largely a technical change that reflects the need to maintain a minimum average daily trading volume for each listed security (which is sometimes otherwise impossible to attain because of liquidity problems).

Among other attributes, the Nasdaq is the most heavily traded market in the world, with average daily volumes frequently in excess of one billion shares and an average dollar value of about $22 billion; compare the Big Board at around 780 million shares and $35 billion in 1998.

TSE 300 COMPOSITE INDEX

Canada's primary stock market index has been in existence for only about 22 years. Introduced in 1977, the TSE 300 Composite is Canada's most widely used market indicator representing 300 of the largest publicly traded companies. When you ask a Canadian, "What did the market do today," you'll be told that Toronto was up or down by so many points. Despite desultory competition from the Montreal Exchange, the TSE 300 is always quoted by the domestic and global media as the definitive, daily snapshot of Canadian market activity. But it is unclear what's next for this index.

There are 14 industry groups (these in turn form TSE sector sub-indexes) and 43 sub-groups included in the TSE 300, which are intended to be reflective of the overall Canadian economy. All the usual suspects are represented from industrials to oil and gas, metals and forest products, communications and media, pipelines and utilities, and financial services and so on. Unfortunately, the index has grown somewhat out of sync with the modern economy. The TSE 300 has the reputation of being a rocks and trees (i.e. natural resource) index, and to a great degree this is still the case. In the early 1980s, approximately 50% of the TSE 300 market weighting was resource based; today, it's under 20%, but that is still approximately three times larger than the leading big-cap U.S. indexes. The Canadian market as represented by the TSE 300 is also very small by world standards, standing at less than 3% of total global market capitalization.

While it is true that the Canadian economy is perceived globally as a commodity play, the reality is that there is only currently one resource stock (Barrick Gold) in the top 10 TSE stocks, and Barrick, it could be argued, is really in the financial engineering business (with its sophisticated gold hedging program and so on). The other leaders are tech (Nortel), telco (BCE, soon to become a .com stock?), banks (the four merger amigos plus Scotiabank), entertainment (Seagrams) and aerospace (Bombardier).

The TSE regularly reviews the 300 and each of its other indexes and follows strict criteria for inclusion and maintenance policies. Unfortunately for the Exchange, however, the scandal resulting from the inclusion of disasters such as Bre-X and YMB Magnex International in the TSE 300 has resulted in a severe credibility problem. It is to be hoped that the new S&P/TSE 60 will reverse this.

Toronto 35 Index
The Toronto 35 Index comprises 35 of Canada's largest companies and represents a cross-section of the major industry sectors. Created in

1987, the 35 was designed to closely track the performance of the TSE 300, but also provide professional traders with the liquidity they needed to be able to transact in entire index baskets (in other words, execute in all 35 stocks simultaneously) as the basis for creating a cash market (stocks), options and futures tripod (see how this works in Chapter 5). It is essential to understand that second and third tier Canadian stocks can be difficult to transact in the size required by an institutional or index mutual fund investor. In turn, the Toronto 35 Index spawned Toronto 35 futures and options contracts as well as TIPS 35, index participation units that have proved popular with retail and institutional investors. As many products, including index-linked GICs, are tied to the 35, its life will probably exceed that of the 300 though that is speculation at this point.

TSE 100 Index/TSE 200 Index

Launched in 1993, the TSE 100 was designed to provide institutional investors with a relevant benchmark against which to measure performance. The TSE 100 represents about two-thirds of the market capitalization of the Canadian equity market and includes 100 of the largest and most liquid stocks traded on the TSE. It comprises four economic sectors: resource, consumer, industrial and interest sensitive. The TSE 200 Index was subsequently designed as the benchmark for mid-cap-to-small-cap stocks within the broader TSE 300 universe. Both indexes have attracted institutional interest and some derivative trading but little else.

The New S&P/TSE 60 Index

The S&P/TSE 60 Index was launched December 31, 1998. It is now widely quoted in the Canadian financial media and elsewhere. As with most other indexes, individual companies play no role in the selection process and are not consulted regarding their inclusion in the index; nor any longer to any great extent is the Toronto Stock Exchange as stock selection is conducted by S&P in conjunction with the TSE Index Committee. Nonetheless, S&P (a division of McGraw-Hill publishing) is largely being entrusted to maintain the integrity of the new index, and listing criteria have apparently been significantly tightened up. In addition, Canadian mid-cap and small-cap indexes have also been created.

The criteria used to determine which stocks are included in the index are primarily market size, liquidity and sector leadership. With 60 stocks, and given the rule of 10—that is, everything in Canada should be about 1/10th that of the U.S.—the new index can be viewed as an S&P 500 equivalent. The S&P/TSE index selection committee also undertakes a rigorous analysis of both the financial and operating condition of eligible companies to ensure their fundamentals are solid. No more Bre-X fiascos is presumably the point here.

The new index has 11 sectors which cover all former 14 TSE 300 sub-groups; the S&P/TSE sector classifications are the same as those employed by the S&P 500 Index. In addition, S&P/TSE 60 companies must also be in the 300 at least for now. The sectors are:

- Basic materials;
- Capital goods;
- Communications services;
- Consumer cyclicals;
- Consumer staples;
- Energy;
- Financials;
- Health care;
- Technology;

- Transportation; and
- Utilities.

S&P/TSE 60—A New Measure of Opportunity?

At time of writing, the stocks in the new S&P/TSE 60 Index are:

- Abitibi-Consolidated Inc. (ticker: A) Basic Materials
- Agrium Inc. (AGU) Basic Materials
- Alberta Energy Co. (AEC) Energy
- Alcan Aluminum Ltd. (AL) Basic Materials
- Anderson Exploration Ltd. (AXL) Energy
- ATI Technologies Inc. (ATY) Technology
- Bank of Montreal (BMO) Financials
- Bank of Nova Scotia (BNS) Financials
- Barrick Gold Corporation (ABX) Basic Materials
- BCE Inc. (BCE) Communication Services
- BCT. Telus Communications Inc. (BTS) Communication Services
- Biochem Pharma (BCH) Health Care
- Bombardier Inc. (BBD.B) Capital Goods
- Canadian Imperial Bank of Commerce (CM) Financials
- Canadian National Railway Co. (CNR) Transportation
- Canadian Natural Resources Ltd. (CNQ) Energy
- Canadian Pacific Limited (CP) Transportation
- Canadian Occidental Petroleum Ltd. (CXY) Energy
- Canadian Tire Corp. Ltd. (CTR.A) Consumer Cyclical
- Dofasco Inc. (DFS) Basic Materials
- EdperBrascan Corporation (EBC.A) Financials
- Enbridge Inc. (ENB) Utilities
- Euro-Nevada Mining Corp. (EN) Basic Materials

- Falconbridge Limited (FL) Basic Materials
- Geac Computer Corp. (GAC) Technology
- Gulf Canada Resources Ltd. (GOU) Energy
- Hudson's Bay Company (HBC) Consumer Cyclical
- Imasco Ltd. (IMS) Consumer Staples
- Imperial Oil Limited (IMO) Energy
- Inco Limited (N) Basic Materials
- Laidlaw Inc. (LDM) Consumer Cyclical
- Loblaw Companies Ltd. (L) Consumer Staples
- Macmillan Bloedel Limited (MB) Basic Materials
- Magna International Inc. (MG.A) Consumer Cyclical
- Mitel Corp. (MLT) Technology
- Moore Corp. Ltd. (MCL) Capital Goods
- National Bank of Canada (NA) Financials
- Newbridge Networks Corp. (NNC) Technology
- Newcourt Credit Group (NCT) Financials
- Noranda Inc. (NOR) Basic Materials
- Northern Telecom Ltd. (NTL) Technology
- Nova Corporation (NCX) Basic Materials
- Petro-Canada (PCA) Energy
- Placer Dome Inc. (PDG) Basic Materials
- Poco Petroleums Ltd. (POC) Energy
- Potash Corp. of Saskatchewan Inc. (POT) Basic Materials
- Renaissance Energy Ltd. (RES) Energy
- Royal Bank of Canada (RY) Financials
- Seagram Co. Ltd. (VO) Consumer Staples
- Shaw Communications Inc. (SCL.B) Consumer Staples
- Suncor Energy Inc. (SU) Energy
- Talisman Energy (TLM) Energy
- Teck Corporation (TEK.B) Basic Materials

- Teleglobe Inc. (TGO) Communication Services
- Thomson Corp. (TOC) Consumer Cyclical
- Toronto-Dominion Bank (TD) Financials
- Transalta Corporation (TA) Utilities
- Transcanada Pipelines Ltd. (TRP) Utilities
- United Dominion Industries Ltd. (UDI) Capital Goods
- Westcoast Energy Inc. (W) Utilities

Failure of the 300 Index—And a New Day for Indexes in Canada

Traders worship liquidity. Remember that liquidity means the ability to transact in size at the bid/ask spread, not just in one or two stocks but preferably in the "basket" of stocks that comprises the major market index. Liquidity is what the Toronto market has lacked, especially compared to the competition coming from U.S. exchanges where so many Canadian issues are interlisted. This has been a real problem for the Canadian market, since many large companies see more trading in their stocks on the Big Board or the Nasdaq in a typical day than they do in Toronto. There's also been a common perception that the TSE 300 is a comparatively easy index to beat since market momentum has usually been sector based (i.e. switching from interest-sensitive stocks such as the financials to cyclicals such as oils or metals). This has been true up to a point, but not necessarily for the reasons adduced. Nonetheless, this perception is one of many reasons why active fund management has been more successful and consequently has had such a strong foothold in Canada. But that is changing, because managers have been having an increasingly difficult time beating the index bogey. The new S&P/TSE 60 Index may change all that. It is more broadly based than the 35 yet should offer the liquidity that the 35 was designed to provide. In addition, Barclays Global Investors are launching and managing new index participation units that track the index, which should give Canadian index investors a new lease on life. British owned and San Francisco based, Barclays Global Investors is a global powerhouse: the world's largest manager of institutional assets and the world's largest index fund manager with assets in excess of C$1 trillion under management in 1,300 index funds in 50 countries worldwide. With the new Barclays Global Investors' "i60" index participation units and recently announced S&P/TSE 60 index derivatives plus the potential for new fund development on the way, things are looking up for Canadian indexers.

It may also seem peculiar that the Toronto Stock Exchange cannot maintain its own index, but as we've seen, publishing behemoths in the U.S. own two of its leading indexes, while in the U.K. the benchmark FTSE 100 is owned by the *Financial Times* group. Certainly the S&P professionals have the credentials to ensure that the composition of the index reflects market reality.

INTERNET SECTOR INDEXES

From the railroads to the Internet, new industries spawn new indexes. While the Internet sector has been strictly a stock-picker's paradise, and consolidation in the industry is as inevitable as it has been ongoing, Internet indexes have inevitably sprung up. New Internet index funds may not be far behind (see p. 80; there are already Internet index options being traded in the U.S.).

The Dow Jones Internet Index
The Dow Jones Internet Index was launched in February 1999 and is comprised of two sub-groups, Internet Commerce and Internet Services, reflecting the basic distinction between the types of companies that are

dependent on Internet business. The Internet commerce group represents companies that derive the majority of their revenues from providing goods and/or services through an open network, such as a website. The Internet Services group consists of companies that derive the majority of their revenues from providing access to the Internet or enabling services to people using the Internet. The index is market cap weighted and currently comprises 40 leading web-related names.

TheStreet.com Internet Sector Index & E-Commerce Index

Hedge fund manager and financial journalist extraordinaire, James Cramer is one of the legends of modern day Wall Street. These indexes are named after his highly popular financial advisory, pay-for-view website of the same name. The Internet index tracks the value of a basket (equal weighting) of 20 Internet stocks (ticker symbol: DOT). Some prominent Net players feature in the index, including Amazon.com and America Online and other high flyers. The e-commerce index tracks the performance of a group of 15 electronic commerce stocks (ticker: ICX). The E-Commerce Index is a more specialized complement to the Internet index and includes names which generate all or a significant portion of their revenue from commerce conducted over the Internet such as eBay, Egghead.com and E*Trade.

MAJOR NORTH AMERICAN
CAPITAL MARKET INDEXES AT A GLANCE

In addition to the U.S. biggies such as the Dow, S&P 500 and Nasdaq, and the familiar Canadian indexes, there is a wide range of other more specialized indexes, both North American and international. They are ranked here approximately by size (i.e. total market capitalization) and degree of specialization.

Wilshire 5000

Tracks practically all publicly traded U.S. stocks. Currently there are about 7,400 stocks in the index (when first introduced, it had approximately 5,000 stocks).

Russell 3000

Measures the performance of the 3,000 largest U.S. companies based on total market capitalization and represents approximately 98% of the U.S. equity market.

New York Composite Index

Comprises all stocks listed on the NYSE (about 2,900 names) organized into four subgroup indexes. Market-cap weighted like the S&P 500 and a widely used indicator of market breadth.

Value Line

Tracks a universe of about 1,700 stocks with the aim of analyzing relative value and ranking each stock for probable market performance out over the next 6-12 months. Forms the basis for the investment recommendations in the widely followed *Value Line Investment Survey*.

S&P SuperComposite 1500 Index
Combines the S&P 500, S&P MidCap 400 and S&P SmallCap 600 indexes and represents about 87% of the total U.S. equity market capitalization.

Schwab 1000
Composed of the 1,000 largest publicly traded companies in the U.S. by market capitalization.

Wilshire 4500
Equals the Wilshire 5000 minus the S&P 500 companies. As is the case with the Wilshire 5000, this index is misnamed. There are approximately 6,700 stocks in the Wilshire 4500; about two-thirds are mid-cap companies.

S&P 400 MidCap Index
Consists of 400 U.S. mid-cap stocks chosen for market size, liquidity and industry representation. Market-cap weighted and one of the first mid-cap indexes.

Amex Composite Index
Covers a range of generally lesser U.S. stocks traded at the American Stock Exchange (home to innovative index participation units such as SPDRs and WEBS). Also where many Canadian interlisted stocks are traded, particularly resource issues.

S&P SmallCap 600 Index
Consists of 600 U.S. small-cap stocks chosen for market size, liquidity and industry group representation. Again, a market-cap index.

Russell 2000

Contains the 2,000 smallest stocks in the Russell 3000 (which contains the 3,000 largest stocks in the U.S.).

S&P BARRA Growth And Value Indexes

Specialty indexes corresponding to two key investment styles: growth and value. Companies in each index are split into two groups based on price-to-book ratios to create growth and value indexes. The value index contains companies with lower price-to-book ratios; the growth index contains those with higher ratios. The S&P indexes included are the 500, 400, Super Composite 1500 and SmallCap 600. The Russell indexes are similarly divided into growth and value. BARRA is a major U.S. quant shop and asset manager.

Nesbitt Burns Small-Cap Index

Canada's own contribution to small-cap indexing. Tracks 400 small-cap Canadian stocks and is widely followed by Canadian institutional investors.

Globe & Mail ROB NETdex

Published by the Globe, NETdex tracks a basket of leading U.S. and Canadian Internet stocks (all the main line names). Priced in Canadian dollars.

International Indexes

- Morgan Stanley Capital International Europe, Australasia, Far East Index (MSCI- EAFE). The premier international market index. Composed of approximately 1,000 stocks traded on 21 global stock exchanges.

- S&P Euro Index and Euro Plus Index. Track the major European markets, including some of the minor countries. Both indexes provide broad geographic and economic diversification through over 11 industry sectors.
- Morgan Stanley's new All Country World Index (ACWI), which combines the EAFE, U.S. and Emerging Market indexes.
- Dow Jones STOXX index co-sponsored by the Deutsche Boerse and the Paris Bourse, a pan-European index. There may soon be more pan-European indexes than European countries.
- Dow Jones Global Indexes. Fairly new indexes that track the stock prices of more than 2,900 companies in 33 countries, 10 world regions, 9 market sectors in 122 industry groups.
- Global Titans, a brand new Dow index that tracks the world's 50 largest companies by market capitalization.

Bond Indexes

- Lehman Brothers Aggregate Bond Index. Covers over 5,000 government bonds, investment-grade corporate bonds and mortgage-backed securities. Most-used U.S. bond index.
- Dow Jones 20 Bond Average. Includes 20 bellwether U.S. utility and industrial bonds (10 utilities, 10 industrials) with varying terms to maturity.
- SCM Universe Bond Index. Definitively reflects the Canadian fixed-income market. Currently comprised of approximately 800 issues representing a full cross-section of Government of Canada and corporate bonds and terms to maturity.

LEADING GLOBAL INDEXES

These are the major world indexes covering the major world stock markets. If you're looking for the Dow Jones Islamic Market Index, presumably you don't need this book.

Europe
- Belgium (Bel-20)
- France (CAC-40)
- Germany (DAX 30)
- Italy (MIBtel)
- Israel (TA-100)
- Netherlands (Amsterdam AEX)
- Portugal (Lisbon BVL)
- Russia (MOS Times)
- Spain (IBEX 35)
- Switzerland (Zurich Swiss Market)
- U.K. (FTSE 100)

Latin America
- Argentina (Merval)
- Brazil (Bovespa)
- Chile (IBB)
- Mexico (IPC All Share)
- Peru (Lima IGRA)
- Venezuela (Caracas IBC)

Asia Pacific/Far East
- Australia (All Ordinaries)
- China (Shanghai B Share/DJ China)

- Hong Kong (Hang Seng)
- Indonesia (Jakarta Composite)
- Japan (Nikkei 225)
- Korea (Seoul Composite)
- Malaysia (Kuala Lumpur Composite)
- Philippines (Composite)
- Singapore (Straits Times)
- Taiwan (Weighted)
- Thailand (SET)

CHAPTER 3

The Indexer's
Arsenal

———

IN THE INTEREST OF BEING COMPREHENSIVE and inclusive, we're going
to look at index investing from the perspective of the primary ways in
which you can be an index investor, not just restricting ourselves to mutual funds. Not all of these products are appropriate for each investor nor
are they equally accessible, since you need a brokerage account to trade
index participation units and even more specialized accounts for index
derivatives. Nonetheless, we'll examine index investing under:

- Index mutual funds sold by brokers, financial planners and direct
  to the investor by banks, trust companies and other independent
  fund suppliers.
- Indexed-linked GICs and other "guaranteed" index products sold
  largely by banks.
- Cash market products such as Canadian, U.S. and international
  index participation units traded on major exchanges and sold
  by brokers.

- Index warrants and notes, which had their heyday in the early 1990s, but represent an interesting, hybrid form of index security.
- Derivatives—primarily U.S. and Canadian index options and futures traded on the principal derivative exchanges.

We'll further break this product cluster down by domestic, U.S. and selected global markets as appropriate. There is little mention of RSPs here, and those three letters sell books, but index investing is an appropriate strategy for all investors regardless of their tax status. After all, an RSP is simply a government-approved, tax-deferred vehicle for holding retirement savings; except for some rules, the assets it contains can be identical to an individual's taxable portfolio or a professionally managed fund. There's a lot of ground to cover here, so the emphasis will be on the features/benefits of each major generic type of index investment product rather than a laundry list of every conceivable index fund or equivalent available to Canadian investors. It is consequently to be hoped that individual investors will know how to use their broker, financial planner or in-branch customer service representative for more information about specific products and/or do their homework either online or through the mounds of marketing literature the banks, fund companies and exchanges produce. While it's invidious, some products are market leaders and some are market followers, so we'll try to focus on the leaders.

As previously noted, the general problem for Canadian indexers to date has been the lack of truly viable index benchmarks (see Chapter 2) coupled with relatively poor performance by the Canadian equity market during much of this decade. While index investing hasn't necessarily been a winning strategy for Canadian investors up until now—and, in fact, it's suffered a bad rap from many financial advisors and market commentators in consequence—that may soon be changing with the advent of the S&P/TSE 60. As a result of the birth of this new index and its sister indexes, the index base for the funds that Canadians have been offered thus far is almost certain to disappear, so it seems pointless to try to make the case for index investing around them.

In the final analysis, the success of any investment strategy—active or passive—ultimately depends on the performance of that strategy versus its relevant market benchmark. At least with index investing, you are killing two birds with one stone. So my response would have to be: since index investing isn't a market timing strategy and since no one can predict future index performance, don't shoot the messenger. For these and many other reasons, U.S. product makes for a much better way to illustrate index principles to say nothing of the compelling underlying investment performance provided by U.S. markets over many years. That's where we'll start.

S&P 500 Average Annual Returns 1973-98

Above all, index investing is non-predictive. The index investor isn't making a bet on certain stocks per se—he/she just knows that he/she has to have exposure to the stock market with some appropriate proportion of his/her assets. Also note that index investing does not guarantee positive results; in some years the index return can be significantly positive and in other years fare miserably:

High: 1995:	37.1%
Low: 1974:	-26.5%
25-year Average:	13.5%

The index movement in the U.S. at the retail investor level began in the 1970s with the Vanguard fund family, the creation of John (Jack) Bogle, a pioneer in the development of no-load, low-cost index products for the equity and fixed-income markets. Vanguard started in 1975 with its first index fund based on the S&P 500, essentially bringing the Wall Street benchmark to Main Street and in the process mounting a frontal attack on the pricing system of the U.S. mutual fund industry. Today, there are about 100 different S&P 500 index funds available in the U.S. If the U.S. index industry has a doyen, it would have to be Bogle, and it's pretty difficult to get away from the dominant position Vanguard has in the market with over 100 funds (20 pure index funds) and almost $500 billion in assets under management.

As noted in the preface, Bogle has just written a compelling new book, *Common Sense on Mutual Funds*, which picks up nicely on the theme underlying the index investing revolution. Harkening back to Thomas Paine and the 18th century American revolution, Bogle writes: "The ills and injustices suffered by mutual fund investors are not dissimilar to those our forebears suffered under English tyranny." What he means specifically is taxation without representation in the form of excessive mutual fund fees.

Given the impact that MERs have on performance, Bogle obviously believes that there is a better alternative to actively managed funds, i.e. index funds, but on the whole he is extremely balanced in his narrative and content to let logic take the reader where he/she wishes to go. But he firmly believes that fund managers must reduce fees to more equitable levels, return to the traditional fund philosophy of long-term investing and limit the asset levels of the portfolios they manage to a size appropriate to their strategies and objectives, all good sound stuff. Surprisingly, but perhaps in the tradition of generals fighting the last war, *Common Sense* makes no reference to SPDRs and their sister products traded at the Amex (see below), which is a curious omission to say the least. Nonetheless, this book clearly reflects the universality of the indexer's creed and is a must-read for serious investors, index or otherwise.

Perhaps what is most important about the U.S. experience is the lessons in index investing principles it can teach to Canadian investors even if our market isn't quite there yet. Smart money isn't dismissive; it's always on the outlook for new opportunities.

INDEX MUTUAL FUNDS

What started in the U.S. in the mid-1970s came to Canada in 1985 with the launch of the pioneering TD Green Line Canadian Equity Fund. Like their U.S. counterparts, Canadian index funds offer one of the most accessible ways to participate in the overall market. To recap, index fund investors have a simple one-stop decision to make; there is no individual stock picking whatsoever involved. Instead, index fund investors buy the "market," gaining exposure to a broadly diversified portfolio of stocks that reflect the major industry sectors of the economy. For simplicity's sake, index investors also have just one number to watch (the daily index level) to keep track of their investment's comparative performance (the more precise number is, of course, the fund NAV; see p. 114). In addition, investors earn the index return (capital growth) plus dividends (this is called the total return) conveniently and accessibly on a pro rata dollar basis. In other words, you can buy exposure to a total market capitalization in the billions for a few hundred bucks.

The most important point about index funds is that while you can't expect to exceed the market return, you also won't seriously underperform the market either. Put another way, index fund investing is non-predictive—you're not presuming to know where the market will go this year and you're not prepared to trust anybody else, including highly trained professional money managers, to make a bet on

your behalf either. Another key benefit of index funds is that they provide the ready-made equity component for your asset allocation strategy, laying the foundation for a well-diversified portfolio. Besides
investment logic, the benefits of index funds or passive management
also include substantially lower fund management fees as we have seen.

In Canada, index investing has been mainly about TSE 300 or Toronto
35 equity index products; in the U.S., it's largely but certainly not exclusively been about the S&P 500. The big banks and trust companies
have several different index funds in their arsenals, usually about the
same range of half a dozen or so funds. Visit your local branch or see their
websites for more information. Interestingly, many of the banks got into
the index fund business originally because they didn't want to pay the
competitive compensation packages the hero managers were earning
in the 1980s at the independent fund companies, which have typically
sponsored active funds. The banks originally began their foray into mutual funds in the area they knew best, short-term savings equivalents,
with the launch of T-bill and other money market funds. But as their
fund assets grew to include other, longer-term fixed-income instruments, they realized they also needed a Canadian equity component
to round out a comprehensive fund family. To their credit, several of
them looked south to see what was happening and came to the conclusion that index investing made sense. Since then, all the Canadian banks
have undertaken a strong indexing mandate, launching a range of equity
and fixed-income index products. While the major banks obviously also
offer actively managed funds (and usually outsource the management
function for them), they have been the prime movers behind the index
investing revolution in Canada, an innovative and highly consumer-
friendly role that bank bashers would do well to consider.

The big Canadian insurance companies have also got into the index
investing game largely as a result of their universal life policies. Universal

life consists of an insurance component and an investment component. The latter must legally be benchmarked to an index, so the money is invested in index "side funds." There are benefits here for the insuree: the gains from the index funds essentially pay for the premiums, while the growth of the index assets is tax sheltered and can be passed on to the next generation tax free. The industry likes to say that Revenue Canada is paying for your insurance with these products. Segregated funds are also creditor proof. In any case, the appeal of insurance that offers both real growth and tax-sheltered growth is substantial and has given another form of impetus to index investing in Canada. The Canadian banks through their insurance arms are also making a push to market universal life insurance.

Another couple of wrinkles you may encounter are so-called "balanced" index or "strategic" index products. All "balanced index" means is that the two conventional components of a balanced fund (equities and fixed income) are passively rather than actively managed. For example, Canada Trust has a Balanced Index Fund which invests in a combination of four existing index funds covering Canadian, U.S. and global equities, and Canadian bonds. "Strategic Indexing," which refers to a relatively new fund family and has actually been trademarked as a brand by the Royal Bank, attempts to amalgamate what are usually seen as divergent growth and value stock selection strategies in one individual fund (the Royal offers three different strategic indexing funds altogether). The Royal's strategic indexing approach applies specific selection criteria to the Canadian and U.S. markets to create a portfolio of stocks with above-average return potential; foreign content is maximized and an active US/C$ hedging strategy is also utilized. Since strategic indexing offers the potential for outperforming the overall market, it isn't pure indexing, but see further *The Sophisticated Indexer*, Chapter 6.

All else being equal, there shouldn't be that much to differentiate among domestic equity index funds, assuming they track the same index, besides these three considerations:

1. Parentage—are you comfortable with the index fund sponsor? A major Canadian bank may be a better bet than a lesser known domestic or international financial institution or fund supplier. Also remember that fund assets are not covered by CDIC (Canada Deposit Insurance Corporation).
2. MERs—generally, the lower cost providers should be the index fund suppliers to consider first. Index funds are basically commodity products and excessively rich MERs really can't be justified.
3. Tracking error—if the index returns 15% and your index fund returns 12%, it's time to ask some questions. After knocking out the MER, see what's accountable for such large (in percentage terms) slippage and select your index fund accordingly.

These are the primary criteria investors should use in evaluating the universe of investable index funds. See below for a select list of Canadian equity index funds ranked by MER, although as noted above this should be one of several considerations in making your choice.

There are 90 odd index funds of all types, including U.S. and international options, currently available to Canadian investors. Something like 25 U.S. index funds are sponsored by all the major suppliers in no-load, load and segregated fund form. Some offer 100% RSP eligibility (a nice trick—in other words, you could have 100% of your RSP invested in the U.S. or other global markets for that matter). How this works and how the fund suppliers get around Revenue Canada is by using Canadian Treasury bills and futures contracts that track the underlying index, U.S. or foreign, instead of directly investing in the actual securities that constitute the relevant index; hence the fund isn't foreign property in the eyes of the *Income Tax Act*. Canada Trust has an S&P 500 clone, AmeriGrowth Fund, which was one of the first of this type, but it's an expensive enough fund (MER 1.37%). The Bank of Montreal equivalent (First Canadian U.S. Equity Index RSP Fund) clocks in at 1.22%, while the TD Green Line U.S. RSP Index Fund is just 0.80%. Many other Canadian-sponsored S&P 500 or international funds use derivatives, too, but this should not be cause for alarm since they cannot employ leverage (see Chapter 5 on how index futures work) in managing fund assets. These include Scotia CanAm Stock Index Fund and CIBC U.S. Index RRSP Fund among many others. In addition, there is a raft of international equity and fixed-income index funds, from Japan and Asia Pacific to Europe and comprehensive international funds, in both cash market (i.e. they hold the actual index stocks) and derivative varieties, some of which are also 100% RSP eligible.

One important thing to watch for with U.S. and global funds is the currency effect, which can create outsized and supra-index returns (example: CIBC U.S. Index RRSP Fund performance in 1998). The weak Canadian dollar amplifies returns, while a strengthening dollar diminishes returns, in which case the fund would experience sub-index performance. The question for the international index fund manager is always, to hedge or not to hedge (i.e. to fix the exchange rate or let it float), and investors should be aware of the way in which his/her fund responds to this conundrum.

Since Canadians are restricted to 20% foreign ownership in registered accounts (such as RSPs and trusteed pension plans), there has been all sorts of effort expended to get around the rules. Generally, financial gurus think that international investing is a Good Thing because of its enhanced diversification, potential for superior performance and returns that for large periods of time have been non-correlative with

North American markets. For a while, as you will recall, Asia was the place to be with double-digit economic growth and stock markets going through the roof in reflection of so much prosperity and productivity. Everybody must choose for themselves, but personally and especially in this market environment, I'd stick to the good old U.S.A. Curiously, I notice Bogle says something about international investing that makes a particular virtue out of necessity for Canadians: "I am not persuaded that international funds are a necessary component of an investor's portfolio...My best judgment is that international holdings should comprise 20 percent of equities at a maximum, and that a zero weight is fully acceptable in most portfolios."

The latest wrinkle in Canada has been the development of so-called "clone" or tracking funds that confer 100% RSP eligibility but are in essence the same as the cash market international fund equivalents offered by the fund sponsor. These products were just approved and are bound to have considerable appeal. Based on much the same logic as the derivative tax ruling (see above), the fund companies involved, which range from AGF to Mackenzie to Templeton, will enter into contractual agreements with the major Canadian banks to "Canadianize" these funds (basically through a swap arrangement whereby the fund agrees to pay the bank a money market yield via a forward rate agreement and the bank borrows an equivalent amount of money to buy units of the foreign content fund). Unlike derivative funds, the clones will be actively managed. It also appears that they'll be charging about 0.50% more in terms of their MER than their corresponding non-RSP eligible funds. It is argued that the problem with international index derivative funds has been tracking error (i.e. the difficulty of ensuring that the index futures positions track their respective global index tightly), but in reality the main problem still appears to be fees; major international index players such as Barclays Global Investors and State Street run billions of dollars in global index portfolios for institutional clients with comparatively little tracking error. Time will tell if even more expensive international product will sell in the RSP marketplace despite its promise of higher returns.

Index funds also have a hidden tax benefit for taxable investors as well as for individuals holding them in tax-deferred accounts such as RSPs, and that is low portfolio turnover (buying and selling of portfolio stocks). Index funds generally only turn over about 5% of the value of their portfolios each year: a) because their mandate is simply to keep up with any changes to their respective index; and b) because they are not chasing hot stocks. This makes the index portfolio very tax efficient since it does not have to realize capital gains the way an active fund with higher turnover would. The net result is that investors' money is compounding longer because it's not paying out (or rather the investor isn't on the hook for) the same level of capital gains tax each year. Of course, investors must ultimately pay the taxperson, but it has been estimated that, over a 20-year time horizon, an actively managed fund would have to outperform an index fund by about 2.5–3 percentage points per year in order to produce the same after-tax returns. In other words, if an index fund returned 10% per year, the actively managed fund would have to return 12.5–13%, which is 25–30% more in order to produce the same after-tax return.

Thus far, we have been considering the virtues of index funds; but they also have, if not vices, then other characteristics that affect their performance. Index funds, unlike actively managed funds, are basically always fully invested. That means for every $1.00 in the index fund, $0.99 or so is invested in equities. By contrast, active funds maintain a cash cushion (for redemptions and as a reserve for new buying opportunities) of anywhere between 5–20% depending on the fund and the market environment. In the event of a market correction, index funds will fall harder than most active funds because of this cash reserve. On the other hand, actively managed funds running large cash positions will underperform on the upside. The trick here is to compare apples with apples. Before making performance comparisons, you should net out the cash position for the actively managed fund and see where things really stand on that basis. As a sidebar, it is also worth asking if it makes sense to pay an active manager as much as 2.50% to manage as much as 20% of the value of an equity portfolio in cash or T-bills.

Trading Notes

Canadian index funds are sponsored by the banks and trust companies and are readily available in-branch, through their online brokerage services or other registered dealers. While Vanguard and other comparable U.S. index funds are not cleared for distribution in Canada, theoretically Canadian investors should be able to hold them through an account with a U.S. discount or Internet broker though there may be negative tax implications in so doing (i.e. potential capital gains liability with the IRS). But there is no U.S. capital gains tax on stocks, bonds or mutual funds taken at source, though there is a 15% withholding tax on distributed dividends.

There is little point in trying to rank the domestic equity index funds by performance because in theory one TSE 300 fund should be about the same as another except for the MER differential (see below for the comparative U.S. story). Also size matters: with an investment of $250,000, some Canadian equity index funds (example: Royal Premium Index) offer an MER of just 0.30%. Others have a $150,000 threshold for similarly good deals (e.g. the premium lines of the CIBC and Scotiabank fund families). For other high rollers, the Bank of Bermuda sponsors a family of global index funds available to Canadian investors called Global Manager (they require a $150,000 minimum investment and they're not cheap in the MER department). Global Manager comes in two forms: pure index (most major global markets but sorry, no Canadian content—too insignificant a market to be included) or leveraged index (so-called "geared"), which means you get twice the play in both bull and bear form. Some of their numbers are outstanding, e.g. geared Germany bull index fund: 47.6% average annual return 1995–98.

Leading Canadian Equity Index Funds and Their MERs*

The two oldest Canadian equity index funds are the TD and Great West Life products, both of which have 10-year plus track records now. While there has been some price-cutting going on, there is still a marked difference among the MERs of the leading Canadian index fund (all TSE 300 unless otherwise noted) providers:

Great West Life Equity Index Fund	2.57%
NN Canadian 35 Index Fund	2.36%
First Canadian Equity Index Fund	1.22%
CIBC Canadian Index Fund	0.90%
Scotia Canadian Stock Index Fund	0.87%
Canada Trust Canadian Equity Index Fund	0.80%
TD Green Line Canadian Index Fund	0.80%
Sun Life Toronto 35 Index Fund	0.70%
Royal Canadian Index Fund	0.50%
Altamira Precision Canadian Index Fund (TSE 100 Index)	0.50%

*Ranked in descending order of magnitude of management expense ratio (MER) as at June 30, 1999.

The Joys of a Competitive Marketplace*

It must be acknowledged that Canadian indexers have not fared as well as their U.S. counterparts in terms of investment performance in recent years. But from this sample of leading U.S. equity (S&P 500) index funds, you can get a sense of how closely competing products track each other in a competitive marketplace (and what a performance it has been):

Vanguard 500 Index Fund	29.0%
DFA Index Fund	28.9%
SSGA (State Street) S&P 500 Index Fund	28.8%
Dreyfus S&P Index Fund	28.8%
Fidelity Spartan Fund	28.7%
T. Rowe Price EquityFund	28.7%

*Ranked in descending order of average annual 3-year returns as at June 30, 1999.

Other Types of Index Funds

The U.S. market provides a true education into the potential of index investing. Beyond the S&P 500 and other comparable big-cap funds, there's lots of choice in terms of more specialized index funds. Some of the major players here include DFA (known as an academic quant shop), Rydex (which sponsors a slew of sector funds) and, of course, Vanguard. The point here is simply to illustrate how indexes immediately lend themselves to new mutual fund development. In addition, brand new (or obscure) indexes soon beget new funds (see below for the coming Internet index fund revolution). There are also quite a few specialist utility, technology and related funds available for investors based on the various sector indexes tracked in the U.S. (see Chapter 6).

For example, in addition to the S&P 500, Vanguard sponsors a Mid Capitalization Index fund (the S&P 400). For small-cap investors, the Vanguard Small-cap Index tracks the Russell 2000. Recently launched, Vanguard's Small Cap Growth and Small Cap Value index funds track the S&P SmallCap 600/BARRA growth and value indexes respectively (see *Deconstructing the Index*, pp. 134 ff.). For investors who are not satisfied with the diversification potential of the S&P 500, the Vanguard Total Stock Market Portfolio holds many of the largest stocks in the Wilshire 5000, which in turn consists of almost every publicly traded equity in the U.S. so it literally can be described as the stock market. For international equities, Vanguard has a similarly constructed index fund called Total International Portfolio.

DFA, which also favours efficient market theory (i.e. you can't beat the market) and is a very low cost, low turnover, diversified provider of index funds like Vanguard, offers a range of funds for investors with substantial resources that track much less familiar indexes and/or market sectors, including the U.S. 9-10 Small Company Fund, which invests in the smallest 20% of companies by market cap traded on the NYSE and in similar sized companies on the Nasdaq and the Amex. Over the last 10 years, the U.S. 9-10 Small Company fund has been top in its class in the U.S. with an average annual return of almost 13%.

There is the whole area of bond index investing as well (see Chapter 6). In the U.S., a number of funds from Schwab, Dreyfus and Vanguard track the Lehman Brothers Aggregate Bond Index and the Lehman shorter-term indexes. In Canada, the range of bond index funds is fairly limited. As we have seen, the SMU Index maintained by Scotia Capital Markets is the primary Canadian fixed-income benchmark. Again, TD was the pioneer in bond indexing in Canada and currently runs one government bond index fund. CIBC has three bond funds which track the more broadly based SMU Index (see Chapter 6). Scotiabank also recently launched its own SMU fund.

Besides U.S. funds, international index funds cover Europe, Asia and so on through the use of derivatives as we have seen, while some invest in physical index securities and others use a combination of both. A common approach is to create portfolio exposure to a specific geographical region via a basket of index futures weighted on some basis: macro-economic factors such as comparative GDP, the market capitalization of the various national bourses or simply on the manager's fundamental outlook for each particular market. This is where you get passive/active management, i.e. where the manager is using a passive index derivative vehicle in the context of an active style. Currency management also varies (i.e. whether the Canadian dollar is hedged or unhedged). Canada Trust's EuroGrowth and AsiaGrowth are examples of global funds managed along these lines.

Breaking News—Index Interest in the Internet

We have already looked at a couple of the current Internet indexes. Now it appears there may be index mutual funds based on some of them. British investment firm Investec Guinness Flight already manages the Internet-based Wired Index Fund and other index funds may be forthcoming. For example, Barclays Global Investors, which is also launching a slew of new sector index products on the Amex (see Chapter 6), has already announced a fund that will track the Dow Jones Internet Index.

Investors may question whether indexing and the Internet will mix. The same key benefits enjoyed by the larger-cap index funds, namely diversification, lower fees and tax efficiency, should obtain. But this is an extremely volatile sector in which investment success has been characterized by a high degree of selectivity in terms of security selection. While all the Internet IPOs coming to market should produce a steady stream of potential index candidates, the M&A and consolidation activity in the sector will also make maintaining an index fund portfolio anything but a piece of cake. The jury's still out on this one.

THE INVESTMENT CONSUMER #1—THE PROS AND CONS OF INDEX FUNDS VERSUS ACTIVELY MANAGED FUNDS

It is time for some balance in this discussion. Since there is no such thing as a perfect investment, each opportunity must be considered on its own merits. Nonetheless (and not withstanding the comment about generally poor Canadian equity index performance during the 1990s) index funds look pretty good on the whole.

Pros

1. Index funds provide highly diversified equity exposure because they track the stocks that comprise the index. Some actively managed funds have much more focused portfolios and are naturally less diversified and consequently riskier.
2. On the subject of risk, index funds enable you to understand precisely what risk you are taking on, i.e. market risk, not the risk of unfortunate/faulty/lucky/highly informed security selection on the part of an active money manager.
3. Index fund fees tend to be considerably lower than their actively managed counterparts. They're also usually no load (a 5% front end load means that only 95 cents on your investment dollar is going to work for you immediately, whereas an index fund gives investors a nice head start by putting 100 cents on the dollar to work the moment you invest).
4. Index funds have significant advantages for taxable and longer-term, tax-deferred investors because of their low portfolio turnover.
5. Derivative-based index funds enable investors to get around the 20% foreign-content limit in their RSPs.

Cons

1. By definition, an index fund will never outperform the market, while actively managed funds can and do. Canada's dean of index funds, TD's Green Line Canadian Index Fund, has a 10-year average annual compound return of just 7.25%, which places it in the third quartile of equity fund performance, well below the average for actively managed Canadian funds. What this tells me, however, is that the Canadian market has been much easier to beat than the larger and more efficient U.S. market.

2. Derivative index funds have tax disadvantages. These funds not only return interest income as income, they also return capital gains as income, i.e. there's no tax break here. The solution: hold them inside your RSP or other registered plan.

3. In general, index funds are much cheaper than actively managed funds, but there are noticeable exceptions which it would be prudent to avoid.

INDEXED-LINKED GICS AND RELATED "GUARANTEED" INDEX PRODUCTS

Index-linked GICs and protected index funds supplied by the major Canadian financial institutions have been designed to appeal to less sophisticated investors by promising to deliver stock market returns with no capital risk. To the extent that they address investors' fears that stocks are a gamble, they're a good thing. Just give some thought to how they actually work (see below and next page) before making up your mind.

Both types of product offer participation in the stock market but with investment principal guaranteed (strong upside/no downside in the jargon). Consider these examples. Scotiabank offers what they term Stock-Indexed GICs which track either the Toronto 35 Index or interestingly a composite of the markets comprising the G-7 economies. With both, your return is equal to the percentage increase, if there is one, of the respective index from issue date to maturity up to a specified maximum (that's catch # 1: many of these products limit your upside potential to less than 100%. For the sake of illustration, say a GIC offers 70% of the market upside. Even if the index goes up as much as 50% during the 5-year term of the GIC, the payout to the investor would only be 35%). If, however, the index produces a negative return by maturity, your principal is nonetheless guaranteed.

CIBC has offered a 5-year protected fund product that guarantees your original investment is 100% protected if you hold it for five years along with unlimited growth potential. There are five no-load funds in this family, including Canadian and U.S. stock, bond and international index products. These funds are fully redeemable and can be sold at any time at current market value but again they must be held for five years for your original investment to be 100% protected. That's catch # 2: tying up your money. There's also a tax consideration with guaranteed products or catch # 3. While they pay no actual interest, you're on the hook for tax on the basis of imputed interest while you hold them, i.e. tax for income you've never seen. As a result, you'd be well advised to keep guaranteed products like this in tax-deferred accounts such as your RSP. Catch # 4 is that you're paying for this protection big time. The MER on these funds (U.S. and Canadian index product) is about 2.85%.

Trading Notes

Protected or guaranteed index products such as these have been around since the early 1990s, when they were first sold institutionally. The basic question is, how do they do it—i.e. how can they invest in the stock market and guarantee your principal at the end of the term? The answer is simple: the bond market (hey, but I thought this was a stock fund?).

In their simplest form, guaranteed index products consist of a strip bond (the principal portion of a bond minus its coupons) and a derivative component. Strips are deeply discounted (at time of writing, you could buy a 5-year strip bond for about 76 cents on the dollar). With the 24 cent difference, the financial institution buys an equity index call option (or purchases, with the intention of rolling them over, index futures contracts) or whatever; this provides the equity exposure. At maturity, the bonds are redeemed at par (100 cents on the dollar) plus any increase in the underlying index as reflected in the value of the equity derivative. This works nicely for the financial institutional sponsor since there's no risk with the bond (it matures at par) and there's no risk with the option contract (if nothing happens with the market, the option expires worthless).

For the individual investor, however, there's opportunity cost to consider. While a guarantee of getting your principal back at maturity may seem like zero downside risk, you should also think about what you could earn by investing directly in the market—or in strip bonds for that matter—on your own. If, on the other hand, the market tanks, you do indeed get 100 cents back on the dollar, but earn no interest or dividend income for the period, i.e. there is no portfolio return. So are you really farther ahead?

Regardless of the specifics of the individual guaranteed products, the major point here is that you can do this for yourself—that is, invest in both bonds and stocks to create the degree of portfolio diversification and risk control that's appropriate for you as an investor (see Chapter 7). That's what asset allocation is all about in the first place. So why would you pay somebody else to do it for you on this hybrid basis?

INDEX PARTICIPATION UNITS—TIPS, SPDRS, WEBS, ETC.

Exchange-traded index participation units (IPUs) resemble stocks in the way they're traded but also resemble mutual funds in terms of their structure. In essence, IPUs give investors the same kind of exposure to their respective index on a pro rata dollar basis as mutual funds, but they have the features of securities proper; mutual funds are really derivative products when you think about it. Unlike mutual funds, index participation units are traded on their respective exchanges like shares, with a bid/ask spread and so on. Consequently, there is continuous pricing for IPUs during the trading day, unlike mutual funds, which are priced only at the close of daily trading. Like mutual funds, IPUs are sold only by prospectus and for a commission through a licensed broker. Most important, index participation units are structured as a trust, with the protection features and so on that implies, generally under the aegis of their sponsoring exchange. Since index participation units are really synthetic securities (they represent a basket of corporate securities but are not themselves corporate securities), investment dealers "create" blocks of units from time to time and therefore ensure liquidity for these products on the floor of the exchange.

Needless to say, all adjustments to their respective underlying indexes (examples: special dividends, stock splits, takeovers, index deletions, additions, etc.) are taken care of by the exchange and are automatically reflected in the current value of the units so there is absolutely no investor risk from changes to the index. Both Canadian and U.S. products are very similar in form, though there are important differences in detail; it may be repetitive, but we'll treat each independently and not assume any carry-forward knowledge through the U.S./Canadian sections.

Canadian Index Participation Units

There have been two highly successful Canadian index participation units to date: TIPS 35 and TIPS 100. The original TIPS actually predate the incredibly successful U.S. SPDRs (pronounced SPIDERS) product (see next page), so here's one for Canadian ingenuity. Featuring a high level of liquidity (investor interest reflected in large trading volumes), both TIPS products have enabled retail and institutional investors to buy or sell the Canadian market with just one trade. Since TIPS hold all the stocks in their respective TSE index—in the same proportion as they are represented in the index itself—the return from TIPS tracks the market tightly, which is not the case with active funds or even index mutual funds for that matter because of the MER differential (see next page). TIPS pay index dividends quarterly and also earn fees from securities lending (also see Chapter 6) and from the interest earned on dividends before they are paid out to unitholders, both of which are in turn passed on to investors, which is not a bad little feature in itself.

TIPS are based on two of the current TSE indexes:

- TIPS 35 (ticker: TIP) track the Toronto 35 Index, which measures the large capitalization sector of the Canadian stock market. The Toronto 35 Index is often called the Canadian big-cap index since it is used as the benchmark for large capitalization equity performance.
- TIPS 100 (ticker: HIP) track the Toronto 100 Index, which measures the large to mid-cap sector of the Canadian market. The Toronto 100 Index is often called the Canadian "institutional" index since many professional pension and mutual fund managers use it as a benchmark for equity performance.

The replacement to TIPS is going to be the new *iUnits* S&P 60 (or i60 for short) sponsored and managed by Barclays Global Investors.

Trading Notes

Both TIPS products are units of a trust that invests in all the stocks that comprise their respective indexes in the same proportion as they are represented in each index. Like stocks, TIPS pay dividends, can be bought on margin and may be sold short. These last two elements give TIPS an element of leverage that obviously index mutual funds don't possess. Each TIPS unit represents approximately 1/10th of the value of the underlying index level. For example, if the Toronto 35 Index level is 400, each TIPS 35 unit would be priced at about $40. The U.S. index participation products work on the same basis. Units trade in increments of $0.05 which is a very tight spread. Unlike actively managed or index fund products, there are no investment management fees associated with holding TIPS so the MER equivalent (essentially the cost of running the trust) is very low at only 0.05%.

While trading these products requires a brokerage account (and brokerage commissions), the cost factor alone should be compelling enough to consider them over other index products. The same is true with their U.S. counterparts. As a footnote, when the two underlying TSE indexes die, then so will TIPS 35 and 100, but presumably they will be replaced with new S&P/TSE 60 Index equivalents.

U.S. Index Participation Units

Not unsurprisingly, the U.S. equivalents of TIPS track the three dominant U.S. indexes:

- SPDRs (ticker: SPY) for the S&P 500 Index.

- Diamonds (ticker: DIA) for the Dow Jones Industrial Average.
- Nasdaq 100 (ticker: QQQ) for the Nasdaq 100 Index.

All three were originally launched on the American Stock Exchange (now the Nasdaq-Amex Marketsite) and have essentially the same structure. Termed tracking stock in the U.S., each product bundles up all the stocks in its respective index into a single share that represents a stake in the unit trust that holds the shares of the companies in the index (the same principle as TIPS) and collects the regular quarterly dividend stream. The trust is a little like an open-ended mutual fund to the extent that it is expandable, i.e. new shares can be created as required. What happens to facilitate this process is that major U.S. financial institutions or brokers will create large blocks of units, a process that requires depositing the index portfolio of stocks with the trust. Arbitrageurs in turn keep the price level of the underlying basket of stocks and the value of the index participation units in sync by taking out any discrepancies between the two as risk-free profit. This entire process is technical, but suffice it to say that there are always shares trading at any given time, and that they are well priced and entirely liquid.

It is for this reason that day traders (short-term market timers) have taken to SPDRs as a means of moving in and out of the market in the way they used to trade OEX index options. It is not that they are no longer trading OEX options, but SPDRs, particularly if bought on margin, also offer leverage (more bang for your buck), but do not suffer from time decay (see notes on index option pricing), which means that if you are wrong about market direction, you won't be immediately punished as index options can do.

Aside from the underlying index they track, the basic differences between the three products centre on how to calculate their price vis-à-vis their respective indexes:

- SPDRs trade at $1/10^{th}$ the current level of the S&P 500. With the S&P at 1300, a SPDRs share would be priced at about US$130.
- QQQ trade at $1/20^{th}$ the current level of the Nasdaq 100. With the Nasdaq 100 at 2400, a QQQ share would be priced at about US$120.
- Diamonds trade at $1/100^{th}$ the current level of the DJIA. With the Dow at 11,000, a Diamond share would be priced at about US$110.

In a similar vein to the range of alternative index products available in mutual fund form from Vanguard and other U.S. suppliers, Barclays Global Investors recently announced that it is planning to launch a series of exchange-traded index funds similar to SPDRs covering some 50 indexes in all, including the S&P MidCap 400, SmallCap 600, S&P 500/BARRA Value, S&P 500/BARRA Growth and other sub-indexes (see *Deconstructing the Index*, Chapter 6), an interesting example of index cross-fertilization.

Trading Notes

The market for the three Amex products, especially SPDRs, is wonderfully liquid. Shares trade in increments of 1/64 of a dollar—that means market impact is slight and is one reason why these products have been taken up by institutional traders who transact them in real size. The point about market impact (measured by the tightness of the bid/ask spread) is that a professional trader will buy or sell more, even if he/she will realize smaller profit opportunities, if the spread is tight. You just trade more often. By the way, the U.S. markets have not embraced decimalization as the TSE has—but with spreads like that on the equivalent of a US$130 stock, you can see why they haven't needed to bother. As with U.S. equity trading in general (except the Nasdaq), a specialist firm facilitates transactions on the floor of the exchange and is responsible for keeping an orderly market in these securities, which is also good for liquidity. Like TIPS, all three products may be bought on margin and sold short. Note that Diamonds pay dividends monthly while the other two trusts pay only quarterly. Lastly, check out the MER equivalent for all three: 0.18%. These products have been cleared for trading in Canada (as have WEBS, see below) and can be easily bought and sold through your broker. Obviously, however, they are foreign property from the point of view of inclusion in RSPs.

Going Global

We've briefly mentioned global index funds (some 100% RSP eligible, some not) available to Canadian investors. But there is another way. The world's most recognized global market index is the Morgan Stanley Capital International (MSCI) country index. WEBS (World Equity Benchmark Shares), which cover 17 different major country markets (from Austria to Australia, the list is quite comprehensive), are based on this leading index and its components. Structured like the other Amex index participation products and managed by Barclays Global Investors, WEBS represent an investment in a so-called "optimized" portfolio of common shares that essentially track the performance of a specific MSCI country index. The point about optimization (see Chapter 5) is that it is sometimes impossible to include and/or trade every stock in a given country's market index because of liquidity constraints. Nonetheless, WEBS do the same job on the international front as the other three do domestically, and feature ease of access to global markets, affordability, flexibility and efficient index tracking. Consequently, WEBS have become one of the best (and cheapest) ways for investors to gain exposure to international markets; they also enjoy excellent market liquidity.

THE INVESTMENT CONSUMER # 2–THE PROS AND CONS OF INDEX MUTUAL FUNDS VERSUS INDEX PARTICIPATION UNITS

Both U.S. and Canadian index funds and index participation units provide accessible and convenient investment exposure to their respective markets along with a high degree of portfolio diversification. In effect, they are one-stop investments. We have also argued that they serve as a more cost-effective alternative to actively managed funds and a more accessible, risk-averse way of participating in the market than buying and selling individual stocks. But there is still a comparative price differential between them along with some other factors that tilt the scales in favour of index participation units for many investors.

Pros

1. Index participation units cannot only be purchased for long-term investment (and even for day trading!), they may also be bought on margin and sold short or used in conjunction with related index derivative strategies (see Chapter 8). With an index fund, you've basically got no choice except being long the fund and have no leverage option (unless you borrow to buy funds). So far as liquidity is concerned, you may buy or sell index participation units at the market at any point during the trading day, while you are stuck with the price of the closing daily NAV for your index fund. Normally, you must also buy or sell your fund by early afternoon at the latest (but again, the price you pay or receive is based on that day's closing values) in most cases.

2. While not as extreme as their actively managed counterparts, index funds can hold assets other than the index stocks (primarily cash, bonds and index participation units themselves). This

could result in a degree of tracking error, which is not the case with index participation units.

3. Index fund investors receive income (in the form of dividends) and capital gains (in the form of market appreciation) from their investment; in non-taxable plans (such as an RSP), these are usually re-invested in additional units of the fund that are credited to the investor's account. Capital gains and income are paid out annually so that the fund itself does not incur a tax liability. Index participation units such as SPDRs and TIPS pay the dividend stream quarterly. All distributions from TIPS also qualify for the Canadian dividend tax credit (of course, there is no U.S. equivalent).

4. These numbers say it all for many investors: 0.05% versus 0.50% in annual MER-equivalent terms, and that's a best case comparison.

Cons

1. The entry level minimum investment for index funds is usually $500 and up, with subsequent minimums as low as $50. There is also no load or commission with most bank or trust company index funds. This makes bank-sponsored index funds extremely accessible for the individual investor. On the other hand, since they are like stocks, index participation units trade in board lots (the most cost-effective unit of purchase) of 100 shares. If the S&P 500 Index is at 1,300, 100 SPDRs would cost US$13,000. However, smaller lots are also tradable.

2. Another obvious point is that to purchase index participation units you need a broker along with a brokerage account and you must pay commissions on purchase and sale.

3. TIPS dividends are paid out at the end of each quarter whereas index mutual fund dividends are reinvested immediately; consequently, IPU investors can face a lag in terms of seeing a return from reinvested dividends although they do receive interest income from the dividends which are sitting in cash during this period.

THE INVESTMENT CONSUMER # 3—PRICE POINT CHECK FOR U.S. AND CANADIAN ACTIVE FUNDS, INDEX FUNDS AND INDEX PARTICIPATION UNITS

Cost is an important factor but certainly not the only factor in making investment decisions. But for price comparison purposes, here goes the MER-equivalent sweepstakes:

U.S.

Average actively managed stock fund:	1.50%
Vanguard 500 Index Fund:	0.18%
SPDRs:	0.18%
WEBS:	1.21% (average)
Closed-end international country fund:	2.09% (average)

Canada

Average actively managed stock fund:	2.25%
TD Green Line Canadian Index:	0.80%
TIPS:	0.05%
iUnits S&P 60:	0.17%
Average derivative global fund:	1.20%

With each of these examples, it is worthwhile considering what would happen if you simply invested in the index and reinvested the MER savings. Over a 10-year time horizon, it has been estimated that an actively managed Canadian stock fund with an MER of 2% is actually costing the investor a little over $18,000 in fees per $100,000 of invested assets so you can see what that would be worth in terms of incremental performance.

INDEX WARRANTS AND NOTES

Index warrants represent a longer-term, option-like index play. There are two types: call warrants (conferring the right to buy the index) and put warrants (conferring the right to sell the index). Index warrants have been created to track various U.S. and other global indexes. One of the big index winners of the early 1990s was a series of put warrants based on the Nikkei 225 Index (the major Japanese market index) underwritten by U.S. and Canadian investment banks. Among the first, as I recall, was one issued on behalf of the Government of Denmark although most of the others were sponsored by investment dealers and banks. A put option gives the holder the right to sell a stock or an index at a certain level; owning a put is equivalent to having a short position (i.e. you are betting that the market will go down), but with much less risk since your potential loss is limited to the premium you've paid for the put (see Chapter 5). Performance in some fund portfolios was saved during that very bad time in the North American markets by the incredible returns generated by these put warrants as the Nikkei crashed from over 40,000 to under 20,000 in a matter of months.

Index notes are another hybrid security that are also children of the early 1990s but still in circulation in the investment world today. Essentially bonds in terms of their credit structure and backed by top-quality issuers (frequently the Canadian federal government or its agencies as well as some of the major banks), index notes promise investors a guaranteed 100% return of capital plus upside potential based on a stock index or basket of indexes. That upside can be as much as 100% (unlike most bank-guaranteed GIC products), but is also frequently less. Unlike bonds, however, index notes pay no interest. Like derivative global index funds, they're also 100% RSP eligible even if the underlying is a U.S. or foreign index. Currently, Canadian investors can choose index notes based on indexes such as the Toronto 35, S&P 500 and Japanese Nikkei 225 as well as other more specialized products that include instruments in bear market form (i.e. the payout is tied to a decline in the market). There is no payout, however, if the index in question fails to perform.

Trading Notes

Warrants have been around for a long time as sweeteners to new stock and debenture issues, but their revival in the index world demonstrates just how versatile derivative-like instruments (which they are) can be. A warrant simply confers on the holder the right to purchase a given security at a stipulated price within a specified time period. They are usually traded in the secondary market (i.e. on the floor of the exchange). To the best of my knowledge, the only index warrant still traded in the U.S. or Canada is a Russell 2000 call warrant.

Index notes are sold by investment dealers and traded in the OTC market; they usually have a $5,000 minimum investment entry level. Like index warrants, they can be sold through a broker at any time prior to maturity but only at current market rates.

INDEX DERIVATIVE PRODUCTS

Index derivatives derive their value from that of their underlying index (hence the name "derivative"). There are two basic types with very different pricing formulas: index options and futures (see Chapter 5). As there are lots of specialized options and futures books, we'll concentrate here on simply enumerating the major products available. I do think, however, that exploring the conceptual basis of index derivative structure and some more sophisticated index strategies are worth taking a look at (also see Chapter 8).

The bottom line with index derivatives is that they have captured the imagination of retail and institutional investors alike. Individual investors use them, index options specifically, as a cost-effective performance vehicle, to gain instant market access and benefit from substantial leverage. Institutional investors use index derivatives (largely index futures but also options) to hedge portfolios, implement asset allocation decisions and generally manage risk, particularly at a time when the P/E ratios of many index stocks are at historic highs. It has been the interplay of both the retail and institutional investor, again in the U.S., that has been responsible for the creation of extremely robust index derivative markets. Suffice it to say that index options and futures are similar to the extent that they provide synthetic exposure to index returns, but that they differ in many important ways; it is vital to be clear about these differences before even contemplating trading them.

Canadian Index Derivative Products

Bad index, bad index derivatives. That in essence has been the Canadian experience to date. Index futures and options based on the TSE 300 were tried starting in the early 1980s and failed. Launched in 1987, the

Toronto 35 Index was created as a new performance measurement benchmark for the large-cap Canadian stock market. The Toronto 35 Index was specifically designed to permit trading in a derivatives tripod (basket of stocks and ultimately index participation units as well as index options and futures). The index options (TXO) worked up to a point, but unfortunately, interest in the futures contract (TXF) never really emerged. In 1998, the TSE did a retrofit with its revised Toronto 35 and 100 index options and futures. Again, their fate will depend on that of their underlying indexes. New S&P/TSE 60 derivative products are scheduled to start trading soon.

Index Options and Futures Contracts

The only Canadian futures exchange that has successfully traded index contracts has been the Toronto Futures Exchange (TFE). Both Montreal and Toronto had a go with index option contracts. Currently, this is the Canadian index derivative offering:

- TSE 35 Index options—based on Toronto 35 as underlying; cash-settled, European-style contract (ticker symbol: TXO). The most liquid index option.
- TIPS 35 Index options—based on TIPS 35 as underlying; cash-settled, American-style contract (ticker symbol: TIP).
- TIPS 100 Index options—based on Toronto 35 Index; cash-settled, American-style contract (ticker symbol: HIP).
- TSE 35 Index futures—based on Toronto 35 Index; cash-settled futures contract (ticker symbol: TXF). The most liquid index future.
- TSE 100 Index futures—based on Toronto 100 Index; cash-settled futures contract (ticker symbol: TOF).

U.S. Index Derivative Products

The Americans discovered index derivatives and have created the best markets in the world in which to trade them. We'll consider how they're used in Chapter 8 and how they're priced (highly simplified) in Chapter 5. For many traders, the OEX contract has been the best day at the track ever devised. Most index derivatives are cash settled (which means that at contract expiry, the difference between the purchase price or strike and the closing price is owed by the seller or short to the purchaser or long); consequently, money, not index stock, is all that changes hands.

Index Options and Futures Contracts

The principal U.S. index derivative exchanges are in Chicago: Chicago Board Options Exchange (CBOE), the Chicago Mercantile Exchange (CME or Merc) and Chicago Board of Trade (CBOT). Besides index options and futures, index futures options (where the underlying is the futures contract itself), are also traded but are not included here. The principal contracts with their ticker symbols and sponsoring exchanges are:

- Dow Jones Industrial Average futures—CBOT (ticker symbol: DJ).
- Dow Jones Industrial Average options—CBOE (ticker symbol: DJX).
- S&P 500 Index futures—CME (ticker symbol: SP).
- S&P 500 Index options—CBOE (ticker symbol: SPX).
- S&P 400 Index futures—CME (ticker symbol: MD).
- S&P 100 Index options—CBOE (ticker symbol: OEX).
- Nasdaq 100 Index options—CBOE (ticker symbol: NDX).
- Nasdaq 100 Index futures—CME (ticker symbol: ND).

- Russell 2000 Index futures—CME (ticker symbol: RL).
- Russell 2000 Index options—CBOE (ticker symbol: RUT).
- Street.com Index options—Philadelphia Stock Exchange (ticker symbol: DOT).

In addition, longer-term options (LEAPS, which stands for Long-term Equity AnticiPation Securities) also trade for the Dow 30, OEX and S&P 500 index products (LEAPS products are listed on the CBOE.) Like shorter-term index options, LEAPS give the owner the right to purchase or sell the index at a specified price on or before a given date up to two years in the future. Unlike index options, but like warrants, LEAPS have a longer life span which makes them more attractive than short-term products that suffer from time decay. In addition, since warrants are not available for the major U.S. indexes, LEAPS provide investors with a warrant-like alternative to index options.

THE COMMISSION OR LOAD FACTOR

To be good investment consumers, we've been focusing on MERs or their equivalents. But there's another cost factor to consider and that is the commission or load payable on acquisition of a fund. Active funds purchased through a broker or financial planner charge a front end or deferred load, usually about 5%. Canadian indexers who purchase funds from the banks and trust companies don't pay loads, which is a key plus for bank-sponsored index products. Brokers typically don't sell index products, but if they do, they get a trailer fee from the fund sponsor in compensation (i.e. the customer doesn't see this but it's part of the fund MER). In the U.S., some index funds actually have loads, but this is really a contradiction in terms, since one of the key benefits of an index fund is low cost. Both exchange-traded index participation units and derivatives bear commission charges which are usually negotiable with your broker (otherwise, use a discounter).

CHAPTER 4

From Wall Street
to Main Street

———

A LARGE PART OF THE IMPETUS towards the development of index products has come from the professional investment community, i.e. Wall
Street itself (I use this term loosely of the entire North American institutional investment community, not just U.S. brokers). This is the case
because indexes have a great deal of relevance to professional investors
and traders for a variety of reasons. Among other things, indexes are the
basis on which they:

- Keep score—fund managers of all types, active or passive, track
  their portfolio returns against the performance of the relevant
  corresponding index(es), i.e. big-cap index for big-cap portfolios, mid-cap index for mid-cap portfolios, etc. Frequently monitored by external performance rating agencies, managers are
  divided into first, second, third and fourth quartiles (first quartile means top 25% of managers) and more precisely into deciles

(first decile means the top 10%) depending on where they place in the index sweepstakes.

- Get paid—virtually all active managers are bonused on the basis of how they perform vis-à-vis the leading equity benchmarks. For some, this is a real gravy train. For instance, in addition to a base fee, hedge fund managers frequently charge upwards of 20–25% of all gains once they have bested the index benchmark return.

- Manage money—managers use indexes and by extension index products for a wide range of investment management functions: price discovery (determining where the market is going); asset allocation (shifting assets from stocks to bonds or vice versa); managing fund assets (using index derivatives instead of managing an actual portfolio of stocks) and a host of other applications.

- Make more money—managers use index products to enhance portfolio returns with rapid-fire index buy and sell programs; employ index arbitrage for theoretically risk-free incremental returns; enter into fee-based securities lending agreements to lend their stocks to managers/traders who must short stock (derivative trading is highly dependent on this capability), etc.

- Measure risk—one measure (but certainly not the best, see Chapter 5) of portfolio risk is based on the index (usually the S&P 500 but it's your choice). Here's how it works: assume the index represents base 1. A fairly "conservative" stock could have a rating of .85; a fairly "aggressive" stock could have a rating of 1.20. What this tells you is that if the index increases 10%, the conservative stock should increase only 8.5% in price, while the more aggressive stock should increase by about 12% (or 20% more than the index move); and vice versa on the downside. This is called "beta" and it's a handy if rough and ready measure of portfolio volatility.

Retail investors are vaguely aware of all this activity and are rightly suspicious of the trading "games" played by professional traders on Wall Street (or Bay Street). But what is important is that this sort of thing has been made possible thanks to the pervasiveness of indexation and the financial technology that has grown up around it. Sometimes individuals—and the press—get it right, and sometimes they don't. Consider: the crash of 1987 was blamed on program (index) trading; it is regularly asserted that quarterly triple witching in index derivatives creates extreme and unnecessary market volatility; when a stock (like AOL) is added to a leading index (such as the S&P 500), journalists note that its price activity begins to bear no relationship to its underlying fundamentals and so on and so on.

But indexing isn't just about games. In the U.S., Canada and other major world markets today, approximately $2 trillion (probably a conservative estimate) of pension and institutional assets are index managed. Leading private and public pension funds have made the switch to passive management for the same reasons that individual investors should consider (see Chapter 1). In so doing, however, the index strategies they are pursuing have given rise to a variety of money-making opportunities for professional fund managers and traders who are there both to facilitate and profit from what the big guys are doing. In this process, much needed liquidity has been injected into the stock market, and we have moved far beyond the time when institutional investors just sat on their assets and the market was only good for a few hundred shares at a go. So are these index "games" games or a reflection of the maturing of the U.S. and Canadian equity market place? Not so long ago, people thought the stock market itself was a "game." You decide.

Be that as it may, and on the basis that what professional investors are doing should be of more than passing interest, we'll explore their use of index strategies to see if we can get a better understanding of how index products work in the real world.

BUT FIRST, SOME MORE HISTORY

As we have seen (Chapter 2), stock indexes were invented in the late 19th century as a measure of daily price movement; hence by extension, market performance. It is important to remember, however, that while index performance was reported daily—just as was the performance of the stocks that made up the index—indexes themselves were not traded. Individual stocks were.

From 1792 (founding of the NYSE) to the 1960s, investors believed (and many still do) that the stock market was a market of stocks, not a stock market. Equally, the stock market in the 1950s and early 60s was largely for the little guy, not for institutions. But the emergence of inflation as a result of the Viet Nam war made institutional investors turn to equities as a store of value for their portfolios (see further pp. 127 ff. on the Nifty Fifty). Previously, corporate pension plans, trusts, endowments and other institutional investors had largely been bond market players, but even the modest inflation of that period gave them a shock as they watched their asset base eroding from capital losses, and real returns from bond yields were slashed (the "real" return is the nominal yield or coupon rate minus the inflation rate).

As the stock market became increasingly institutionalized in the 1970s, pension and mutual fund managers required a mechanism for buying and selling large amounts of individual securities; hence block and then liability trading, in which an investment dealer facilitates institutional clients by agreeing to buy or sell large amounts of stock as principal, was born. Previously, brokers worked on an agency basis in which they risked no capital of their own; they simply bought and sold at the market on behalf of clients and collected their fixed (until May day 1975 in the U.S. and 1983 in Canada when they became unregulated) commissions in the process. As an aside, it is also from these principal trading roots that the famous "bought deal," in which a dealer signs the cheque for an offering of corporate securities and then hopes to be able to peddle the wares through its own distribution system or through a syndicate of other brokers, emerged. From block trading individual equities to block trading a basket of stocks that basically reflects the composition of the overall index is not a large step, and institutions became increasingly interested in buying and selling the whole market as the theory of modern portfolio theory and the accompanying rise of asset allocation strategies took hold.

Asset allocation research, which has its beginnings in pension plan performance studies, demonstrated that appropriate asset class exposure is much more important to long-term investment performance than individual security selection. Scholars argue about the exact number, but in a famous study it was concluded that something around 90% of the variability of investment returns from various portfolios is attributable to managers' long-term asset allocation decisions with less than 5% resulting from superior securities selection and market timing. Hence the question for the pension manager increasingly became not what stocks should the fund buy, but how much stock market exposure should the fund have. The growth of indexation, by which the fund simply seeks to mirror the market and constructs a portfolio of individual stocks based entirely on their index weightings—not on the basis of any conscious attempt to outperform—soon became more than just a topic for learned financial journals. Because it was the obvious way to implement asset allocation decisions, it was also clearly the way to make money. Then a new development occurring almost simultaneously on LaSalle Street in faraway Chicago showed Wall Street the way.

Stock options began trading in Chicago at the CBOE in 1973. While options markets had existed for years (through an unregulated OTC market in New York that was probably as crooked as any market can be; options, by the way, used to be called "papers" on Wall Street. For more on this and other nuggets, see the classic *Where Are the Customers' Yachts?*, surely the most charming book about the business of broking stocks ever written.) 1973 was different, however, because of the pricing formula that went with it (see Chapter 5). From individual stock options to index options took a very short time indeed, and starting in the early 1980s it became possible to buy or sell the entire market with just one transaction, not 500 different ones, thanks to the simplicity, convenience and cost-effectiveness of index options and futures.

The benefits of index derivatives as a means of trading and hedging the market or individual stocks also immediately became clear. In particular, derivatives offered a significant cost advantage over trading individual stocks as they are cheaper to transact from a commission, bid/ask spread and market impact standpoint. Index products are also much easier to trade and offer a higher degree of flexibility and liquidity than transacting in baskets of underlying stock.

Equity index derivatives have since become among the world's most heavily traded financial instruments, readily surpassing the value of the underlying securities that make up their respective indexes. Today, it is estimated that the dollar-equivalent value of U.S. equity index derivative trading is about 1.3 times greater than that of all American exchange trading in the underlying index securities themselves. This phenomenon has been jocularly referred to as the tail wagging the dog. Other key contributions of index derivatives have been to make it possible to price market and security-specific risk much more effectively and to create a price discovery mechanism that operates even before the market is open in the morning.

The rest, as they say, is history with literally trillions of institutional dollars now committed to index investing in the U.S. Studies of the institutional investment community in Canada confirm the U.S. experience. In 1998, 21% of Canadian pension funds indicated that they were employing passive management for at least a portion of their domestic equity fund holdings; 17% were indexing their bond assets. These numbers are up sharply from 1995 and will almost certainly continue to grow going forward. In addition, many pension funds are currently employing simulated index strategies (paper trading), but are expected to be coming on board over the next year or so. The momentum is strong in terms of indexing not just the Canadian but also fixed-income, U.S. and global markets. As passive management is estimated to cost the pension plan sponsor about one-third the price of active management, there is good assurance that this trend will continue.

Just How Much Does the Tail Wag the Dog?

Global data collected by the Bank for International Settlements (BIS) based in Basel, Switzerland as at June, 30 1998:

Total value of all derivative contracts outstanding:	US$72 trillion.
Total value of U.S. GDP (Gross Domestic Product):	US$8.8 trillion.
Total trading on the NYSE for 1998:	US$7.3 trillion.

GAMES (ACTIVE) MANAGERS PLAY

Before we consider index-related gamesmanship, it might do to reference some of the tricks of the trade available to active fund managers.

First of all, it would be naïve of investors to think that what a fund says it is going to do in its prospectus or marketing bumpf is precisely what it always ends up doing. We have already referred to the case of the post-Lynch Fidelity Magellan fund, which made a big bet on interest rates and became embroiled in the bond market meltdown of 1994. Investors who bought Magellan and who had read the prospectus or followed the periodic disclosure of fund holdings were almost certainly aware that the fund could and would hold fixed-income securities. What was shocking to unitholders was the fund's level of exposure to the bond market, not that bonds were in the portfolio. The same situation obtains in Canada, where major equity funds regularly commit assets to the bond market opportunistically in the expectation that they can goose returns or increase their cash holdings if they are unsure/afraid/numbed by the current state of the equity market. Investors nonetheless are paying active equity managers to run fair-sized bond and cash portfolios indirectly, which may not exactly be their area of specialization.

This is one of several recognized ways that Canadian active managers can beat the TSE 300. If the market is flat, it's probably a good strategy because bonds pay regular, semi-annual interest, income that's also a lot higher than dividends. Similarly, active managers will overweight industry sectors (that is, hold more than the index weighting in appealing industry groups. Example: in a declining interest rate environment, smart money owns the banks no matter how expensive they appear to be; not doing so is what's hurt Altamira and Trimark in recent years). Another way of beating the index is holding U.S. or foreign stocks up to the 20% permissible limit, which usually means injecting superior international market performance into a basically Canadian (and underperforming) portfolio.

These techniques are all well and good if they make people money and make their managers look good (example: "window dressing" at quarter-end, the ritual whereby active managers ensure that the quarter's hot stocks are included in their portfolios even if they have been purchased in the last month or the last week). But surely it is not unreasonable for investors to wonder whether they should be giving their money over to a sort of "blind pool" in which the manager takes a shot at what's moving as opposed to following the explanation of the strategy of the fund as numbingly and legalistically inscribed at the beginning of the prospectus, i.e. the fund investment objective. In other words, if an investor thinks he/she is investing in Canadian equities, then shouldn't the fund invest pretty much exclusively in Canadian equities? Otherwise, you are paying for expertise that many active managers simply do not possess. Ultimately, your only true guarantee of knowing precisely what you are purchasing is by investing in an index fund or equivalent, but even there there's some room for ambiguity (see Chapter 6).

For our last trick, recall the chart at the beginning of Chapter 1, which depicts the octane rating of two popular kinds of gasoline (i.e. the 5-year performance of a prominent actively managed Canadian mutual fund versus the TSE 300). What this actually illustrates is known in the business as "closet indexing," the propensity of active managers to (consciously) mimic the market weightings of the index in their portfolios. Many active managers are still in the (index) closet for a reason: their jobs. When a stock is on a tear, its quoted value increases and so does its weighting in its respective index. The active manager and his brethren have no choice but to buy more, the manager's portfolio more and more resembles the index, and pop goes the TSE or the S&P or whatever. Which takes us full circle.

GAMES (INDEX) MANAGERS PLAY

As we have seen, sophisticated pension funds and institutional investors have turned to index investing for a wide range of reasons: lower transaction costs, lower market impact costs, lower portfolio turnover, etc. But there always has to be the "other side" of the trade to enable them to fulfil their objectives. That other side could be another institution, a broker/dealer, an independent floor trader or even you. As a consequence, new institutional/pro trader strategies have emerged that definitely impact market volatility though not necessarily in the negative sense ascribed to them by the popular press. In fact, good money can be made from market volatility (example: shorting premium-rich index call options). But to repeat our theme, understanding what Wall Street is up to is probably in every investor's self-interest.

Buy and Sell Programs

The NYSE defines program trading (buy and sell programs) as including a wide range of portfolio strategies that involve the purchase or sale of at least 15 stocks with a total market value of $1 million or more. In practice, the programs are much larger, usually involving all the stocks (or a representative number in an optimized portfolio—see Chapter 5) in a particular index, most frequently the S&P 500 or Nasdaq 100. Programs are big business on the Big Board, accounting for just under 20% of average daily NYSE trading volume and worth something like $7 billion each and every trading day.

There is no mystery about buy or sell programs; they mean exactly what the words say. While program trading strategies are used for a wide range of trading and portfolio management functions, they all essentially involve just three things: buying the basket of index component shares, selling the basket of index shares or selling the basket short.

Frequently, sell programs in New York are experienced at the close of the trading day at 4:00 p.m. (on close orders), buy programs at the opening. In either case, program trading permits the implementation of a market view that may be portfolio based or simply speculative. It is entirely up to what the end-user has in mind. As institutional investors and traders are just like anybody else, they tend to like to see the market confirm the wisdom of their actions or point of view. If they are bullish generally or have added to their portfolios on a given day, they would obviously be happy for the last trades in the index stocks to close at or near their intraday highs. It is entirely possible, through a program trader at one of the investment dealers, for a professional investor to use program buying to ensure that there is a strong finish to the trading day and consequently to his/her portfolio valuation level. Similarly, if a particular industry group looks weak—earnings worries, new product delays, whatever—sell programs can be implemented either in the cash market or more likely through index derivatives, which enable the manager to reduce exposure to the sector without having to sell the underlying stock.

Buy or sell programs on their own are basically random and unpredictable, but what's going on in the index derivative market can serve as a leading indicator of future market action because it is integral to the use of program trading. For example, the block index options market in the U.S. is dominated by institutional traders (we're talking about thousands of contracts per trade here, not the usual five or ten lots individual investors speculate in). If a trader sees that a large block of OEX call options has just been purchased, that is bullish because whoever sold the options will have to buy the index basket of stocks via a program trade to maintain a risk neutral position. There's no real possibility of front running (profiting from knowing how a previous trade will impact the stock or index price on the next trade) because the two transactions are usually effected simultaneously. Similarly, if the trader sees a large block of put options being purchased, that's bearish because the seller will have to go out and short the index basket (sell program). Index futures can achieve precisely the same result often cheaper and faster. For example, if an institution buys SPX or NDX index futures and in so doing bids them up above fair value, somebody else is going to sell futures and buy the index stocks, thereby also bidding up the basket of stocks (temporarily at least); there's more on how this form of arbitrage works in Chapter 5.

In all of these cases, there is no question that the programs (legally) affect security prices. The proof is in the liquidity pattern of the index stocks themselves. Index stocks on the Big Board can move entirely because of a buy or sell program in the absence of any other news or fundamental development. Once the program is over, however, either the bid dries up or the offering disappears except by way of a relatively small number of shares. In essence, the programs are a sound and fury sort of situation in which price movements can be achieved almost instantaneously and on relatively little volume; then the market mysteriously settles down again. Once more, this is a function of liquidity or the comparative lack thereof. The occasional illiquidity of a market as massive as New York is a marvel to most people, but don't forget that the specialist who makes markets in the individual index stocks on the floor of the exchange is only "good" or on the hook for 2,099 shares at the posted bid/ask spread (which is to say that only 2,000 shares constitute the market for a given stock; the additional 99 shares are for odd lots. And that's only for the big stocks, too). That means that, at an average price of about US$45 per share, you can theoretically move the market in a major NYSE stock for as little as US$90,000—which is not very much in the overall scheme of things. But we digress.

For those concerned about the morality of buy and sell programs, don't forget that nobody seems to complain when buy programs help jack up stock prices. In addition, these programs are essentially speculative and can and do produce losses for the individual traders involved, except when they are arbitrage (riskless) trades, in which case they hurt nobody. If you're looking for a culprit, blame the computer, which enables simultaneous execution in the basket of index stocks at the prevailing bid/ask spread (there was talk of banning the telephone from the floor of the Big Board for similar reasons in a pervious era).

The NYSE has long been concerned with assessing the impact of programs on the normal functioning of the market particularly in light of the fact that they have been blamed in the media for excessive market volatility. In response to the severe market corrections in October 1987 and October 1989, the Big Board instituted "circuit breakers" to reduce market volatility and promote investor confidence. As the name implies, circuit breakers originally halted trading for one hour if there was a 250 point drop in the index and for two hours with a 400 point decline. In 1997, the circuit breaker policy was liberalized, with trading halts of 30 minutes and one hour for 350 and 550 point declines respectively. If triggered in the last 30 or 60 minutes of the trading session, the market was to be closed until the next trading day. Circuit breakers were triggered for the first and only time on October 27, 1997, when the Dow fell 350 points at 2:35 p.m. and 550 points at 3:30 p.m. That reflected an approximately 7% overall decline and shut the market down for the remainder of the day.

Early in 1999, the NYSE implemented new rules to be calculated quarterly as 2% of the average closing value of the Dow for the last month of the previous quarter, rounded down to the nearest 10 points, and implemented as follows:

- A decline in the Dow of the predetermined 2% value requires all index arbitrage sell orders of the S&P 500 stocks to be stabilizing, or sell plus, for the remainder of the day, unless on the same trading day, the Dow advances to a value within one-half of the two percent below its previous day's close.
- An advance in the Dow of the predetermined 2% value requires all index arbitrage buy orders of the S&P 500 stocks to be stabilizing, or buy minus, for the remainder of the day, unless the Dow retreats to a value within one-half of the two percent above its previous day's close.
- The restrictions are re-imposed each time the Dow advances or declines the predetermined amount.

Accompanying this change, the NYSE also eliminated the so-called "side car" provisions, which went into effect when the S&P 500 futures dropped 12 points (about 96 Dow points) from the previous day's close. The side car had diverted program trading orders into a separate file for five minutes and banned the entry of certain types of limit orders for the remainder of the trading day.

So there you have safeguards for buy and sell programs that are currently in place at the Big Board.

Cold Comfort? The New NYSE Collars

- A 1,000-point drop in the Dow before 2 p.m. will halt trading for one hour; for 30 minutes if between 2 p.m. and 2:30 p.m.; and have no effect if at 2:30 p.m. or later.
- An 1,950-point drop before 1 p.m. will halt trading for two hours; for one hour if between 1 p.m. and 2 p.m.; and for the remainder of the day if at 2 p.m. or later.
- A 2,950-point drop will halt trading for the remainder of the day regardless of when the decline occurs.

As noted, technology makes buy and sell programs possible because index baskets can be processed electronically. The SuperDOT system is the NYSE's proprietary electronic order routing system that permits NYSE member firms to transmit market and limit orders directly to each trading post (or station) on the exchange floor where the index securities are traded. After the order has been completed, a report of execution is returned directly to the member firm office over the same electronic circuit that brought the order down to the floor in the first place. What this means is that SuperDOT, which can currently process about two billion shares per day, will deliver fills for an entire index basket of stocks up to a certain dollar amount simultaneously and instantaneously. Today, program trades can be executed almost literally at the touch of a mouse and that, more than anything, is what scares people.

Portfolio Insurance

Portfolio insurance (or PI as it used to be called) was interred either late in 1987 or early 1988. No one today can remember the way to the cemetery. Widely blamed for its part in the massive 22.5% market meltdown on October 19, 1987, portfolio insurance is really only a subset of program trading but it's been a contentious one.

The theory behind PI was that dynamic hedging (sometimes called tactical asset allocation) could protect a portfolio cheaper, faster, better than the old-fashioned buy and hold strategy of professional investors in the 1950s, 60s and 70s, when asset allocation meant going from 50% stocks/45% bonds and 5% cash to 49% stocks/46% bonds and 5% cash as market conditions changed. In other words, the old school manager would just hunker down during a bad market and hope for the best. What's more, academic research was beginning to show that you could significantly improve overall portfolio returns (by one hundred basis points, i.e. one percentage point, or even more) by using a tactical approach. PI offered the best of both worlds. You didn't need to sell your stocks at all; instead, you sold index futures (remember, the right thinking portfolio manager is running an index fund). In this way, if the cash market (your actual stocks) went down in value, your short futures position would correspondingly increase in value, thus neutralizing any losses. The net result is that you would have created a form of insurance policy for your fund that would be much cheaper than paying brokerage commissions on the wholesale elimination of equities from your portfolio.

That in any case was the theory. Massive amounts of PI-related portfolio "overlays" as they were termed were created for U.S. pension and other institutional assets, and everything should have been okay until the actual insurance was put to the test. But in October 1987, when everybody was heading for the door at the same time, the programs simply ceased to function and the whole (largely academically inspired) thing was shown to be something of a joke. But ultimately, PI was let down by its lowest common denominator. If a portfolio manager sells futures against an index or even an actively managed equity holding, someone else has got to buy them. That individual is typically a floor trader at the Merc in Chicago (the world's senior index futures exchange). In turn, the floor trader doesn't want this liability, and in fact treats it like a hot potato, so he will then hedge his position by selling stocks short in the cash market (i.e. New York). That was the way it was supposed to work up to Monday, October 19, 1987. But guess what? That day the cash market for the underlying index stocks (only good for 2,099 shares at the bid/ask at the best of times) dried up. The specialists were not answering their phones. There was no bid. There was no market. The intermarket glue that bound the equity and futures markets together had become unstuck at its most sensitive and human point. RIP portfolio insurance.

Triple Witching

Triple witching refers to the concurrent, quarterly expiration of stock and stock index options and index futures contracts which takes place four times a year during the last trading hour on the third Friday of March, June, September and December in Chicago and New York. Usually a recipe for market volatility, every time triple witching comes around there's a tremendous flurry of activity on Wall Street as the pundits try to figure out which way expiry will take the market. Since they're usually more often wrong than right, many traders elect to sit out the session altogether. This is almost certainly your best strategy because it's a mug's game trying to figure how the dust is going to settle on expiry Fridays.

The central point about triple witching is that it is inevitable: futures prices must "converge" (that is, precisely match the cash market index price—see Chapter 5) and options must expire because these are the fundamental characteristics of both types of derivative product. But if it is inevitable, that's the only thing that is predictable about quarterly expiration. The other point about triple witching is the extremely heavy trading volumes that are generated both at and pre-expiry as the complex of stock options and stock index futures and option positions is unwound. For instance, the June 18, 1999 expiry saw 345 million shares change hands during the first hour of trading at the NYSE, the largest volume in history for that time frame (345 million shares used to be a very good entire day's trading).

While many traders have already covered (reversed or flattened out) or rolled (extended to future monthly expiries) their stock and derivative positions before triple witching, some nimble of foot insist on trading right to the bitter end. This can be very dangerous as many traders who have been short premium (for instance, traders who sell out-of-the-money OEX call options close to expiry in the expectation that they will expire worthless, i.e. they will get to keep the premium for nothing) have discovered when the market suddenly ramps in the last half hour of the trading day. Conversely, traders will buy cheap near-the-money index calls just prior to triple witching simply as a form of gambling. It's a calculated risk: if it works, it works, if it doesn't, it doesn't. On a somewhat related point, I can recall a TSE floor trader who late in a trading session loaded up on very cheap puts of a stock that was the subject of an extremely complicated lawsuit. That very night after the close, the court released its opinion in favour of the trader's position; he had scored massively and wasn't seen for months.

The key thing to understand, however, is that index derivative contracts themselves aren't responsible for market volatility; it's the accompanying offset trading in the underlying index stocks which is. Don't forget that, every time a trader buys or sells a contract (let's say an OEX index option), somebody else has to take the opposite side of that trade. That position in turn has to be hedged, usually but not always in the cash market, i.e. by an equivalent, offsetting stock position. That's what can cause the volatility: rapid-fire program buying or selling of the 100 stocks that comprise the S&P 100 to hedge index derivative positions.

Arbitrage

In the investment business, arbitrage generically means getting something for nothing. In the good old days, it was based on intermarket inefficiency: for instance, selling the same stock in New York for 25 cents more than it could be bought in Toronto. So-called "risk arbitrage" (buying a stock in expectation that it is going to be a takeover candidate) as practised by stock raiders (this is what Boesky said he did for a living) is ill-named because pure arbitrage involves no element of risk. Typically today, however, arbitrage means index arbitrage, which involves the purchase or sale of a basket of stocks in conjunction with the sale or purchase of a derivative product, such as index futures, in order to profit from the price difference between the two. This happens in the market more frequently than one would think, and because you're both long and short the same underlying security, your position should be risk neutral and generally is.

On the analogy of triple witching, if futures are "cheap" (i.e. trading at a discount) relative to their underlying index stocks, a trader will buy the futures and short the basket of stocks in the knowledge that at expiry the derivative and cash market prices will converge (see further p. 119). The risk-free profit is the relative cheapness of the futures contract; to make any money, however, a trader would have to do this in size and as frequently as market conditions permit. On this note, traders are usually characterized as having monstrous appetites for risk, gambling large sums on the swings and roundabouts of the market. This is true up to a point, but a fair chunk of their income comes in a very benign form: interest.

When you declare a short sale (your assumption is that the stock will go down and you will be able to buy it back later at a lower price; to do this, you must borrow stock through a process known as securities lending; the stock is then hypothecated and you are on the hook for any price increase that may occur; you are also on the hook for paying the beneficial owner of the securities any dividend income that is due), the money is deposited directly into your account. With index arbitrage, in which the short sale could include as many as 500 stocks at current market values, the amount of money in question and the interest it earns even for a short period of time can really add up. Similarly, index futures traders are sitting on large piles of cash (usually T-bills) as margin for their index positions. For many traders, interest income is a very important component of their overall compensation.

While index arbitrage helps traders make money, it also serves as a market corrective. For instance, if there is price discrepancy between the market price and net asset value of index participation units such as SPDRs or QQQ, a large institutional investor would buy the so-called "tracking shares" and turn them over to the trust, receive the underlying stocks in return and sell them into the market at the prevailing market price, thereby capturing this differential. This type of arbitrage is obviously not something the average investor could do, but it does illustrate the arbitrage mechanism by which markets quickly revert to "fair value." The same is true with the futures example considered previously; futures prices won't remain cheap for long once everybody starts putting on the same arb.

Price Discovery

Even for traders or portfolio managers who are virulent anti-indexers and concentrate solely on following individual stocks, what the market itself is doing and is going to do is of more than passing interest. There are various index tools managers use for their predictive value. Index futures are extensively employed as a forecasting device in both the bond and stock markets. The 30-year U.S. treasury bond future and the S&P 500 index future market quotes are inevitably displayed prominently on any serious trader's screen. Since the value of a futures contract rises and falls based on what traders are willing to pay for it at any given moment (remember that the contract is settled at a future date), there's an old adage in the business that "futures lead cash." What's more, academic studies have found that during the trading day, the futures index leads the cash market index by an average of about five minutes.

Even before the opening bell in New York, a similar but less predictable relationship exists thanks to overnight trading in the Globex futures contract (the S&P 500 traded on the Globex exchange system) in Asia and Europe while the U.S. is still asleep. Globex is the first thing U.S. equity traders pay attention to when they get to their offices in the morning. The predictive value of the Globex contract is based on the concept of fair value (see Chapter 5), which market pros use to get a sense of which way the market will open.

Futures traders are usually students of both fundamental and technical analysis (i.e. charting), as well as so-called "intermarket" analysis, which explores the relationships between bond and stock prices, and between commodities and industry sectors and other inter-relationships. The important point is that the futures market is as close as you can get to a free auction market, in which complete information is instantaneously disseminated. In this regard, the frenzied futures trading pits stand in ironic contrast to the more sedate stock market, where prices can move on insubstantial, unsubstantiated or sometimes no information at all.

Pop Goes the Index

When a stock is included in a major index for the first time, there's usually a rash of market activity simply because everybody who runs index money has gotta have it. As a result, and curiously enough, the inclusion of a new index stock provides a chance for some active fund managers to beat index managers at their own game. As we have seen, if new S&P 500 company X represents 0.x% of the index market cap, then index fund managers must ensure that it represents 0.x% of their total index portfolio holdings.

As a case in point, consider what happened when America Online (AOL) was added to the S&P 500 Index effective December 31, 1998. Of all the Internet-related companies in the U.S., few have had the run that AOL stock has enjoyed, up over 500% in 1998 alone. Just prior to its inclusion in the index, AOL was trading at an all-time high of

US$141. Since on inclusion AOL would comprise about 0.6% of the S&P 500's then-total $9.7 trillion market cap, a fund such as the Vanguard 500 Index fund needed to match that market weighting, which in this particular case worked out to purchasing about three million shares worth some $420 million. While normal index manager practice is to trade index additions and deletions over a certain amount of time to minimize market impact costs, all that AOL stock was bought by Vanguard on one day before the close on December 31, 1998.

If the market maxim for successful investors is supposed to be, "buy low, sell high," indexers are frequently obliged to buy high as a matter of course because they don't have the luxury of planning the timing for their trades. Ironically, active managers can benefit from this situation because outperformers like AOL, which perhaps helped them beat the index on the way up, now provide them with the opportunity to cash out at near all-time highs and get back in later at lower prices. It is common knowledge that new index stocks invariably sell off just after the index effect wears off.

The index feeding frenzy doesn't always work this way, however. During June 1999, Ascend was removed from the S&P 500 once its merger with Lucent was consummated. There was plenty of speculation as to its replacement in the index. What pro traders would be looking for is a stock that was approximately the same size by market cap (possibly an S&P 400 stock ready to climb up to the 500 club) with plenty of liquidity and in an industry something remotely like Ascend's. There were plenty of candidates and the tech sector generally rallied sharply during the week or so before the end of the month possibly on the basis of its own momentum but also in part in anticipation of this event. Nonetheless, the new replacement turned out to be a sleeper and its stock closed up only fractionally on the day it joined the exclusive S&P 500.

The same phenomenon is observed with the annual June revisions to the small-cap Russell 2000 as companies exit that index and ascend the food chain to the Russell 1000 (recall that the Russell 2000 comprises 2,000 of the 3,000 largest U.S. stocks; the Russell 1000 reflects the top one-third). Each year, a substantial portion of the Russell 2000's total market capitalization and billions of dollars exit the index, resulting in some discernible volatility. Typically, traders to go long the additions to the index and short the deletions, since they know what's going to happen. As the Dow changes so infrequently, it is not really subject to these same pressures, but in Canada, the TSE 300 annual index revision in February and periodic revisions throughout the year can cause much the same effect. When index money speaks, the market listens.

At the end of the day, index "games" exist and there is nothing any one can do about them. In the late 1980s, when everybody was looking for a sacrificial lamb for the market meltdown in October 1987, program trading took it on the chin. The big U.S. dealers declared a self-imposed moratorium on program trading for their own accounts (they would, however, still execute for clients) in the hope that the PR value of this move would help calm the markets. Needless to say, the ban did not last long. What is interesting about making portfolio insurance the scapegoat for the crash of '87 is the facts. Despite the fact that the U.S. long bond was yielding almost 10% and the S&P 500 trailing P/E multiple was well over 20X in October of that year—by any historical measure, a recipe for disaster—it is clearly so much more reassuring to blame new financial technology rather than fundamentals for market declines.

Since index "games" are played, the intelligent investor should be apprised of what they are and how in a general way they work. But if pro and institutional index trading has conferred one key benefit on the market as a whole, that would have to be the high degree of liquidity or ease of trading now present. When I started to watch the market carefully, the average daily volume at the NYSE was less than 100 million shares per day. Today, it's running at just under a billion on a good day. Liquidity is an essential aspect of risk management because it means you can cash out your equity when you want to and not bring the entire market down in the process.

CHAPTER 5

The Language
and Mathematics of
Index Investing

———

A CURIOUS BUT NOT UNEXPECTED by-product of the index investing revolution has been the invasion of academics, particularly Ph.Ds with physics backgrounds, into the trading rooms of the major investment houses as well as on the buy side (pension and mutual fund management) of the Street. I know one eminent bond meister whose academic background is marine biology; previously he worked for the federal government's fisheries department as a quantitative scientist. Presumably discerning patterns in the bond market is much easier, and infinitely more rewarding, than trying to guestimate how many cod are left in the North Atlantic.

This intellectual firepower in part explains why Wall Street has embraced passive investment management, but the deeper reason lies in the arcana of financial science, which as a science is recent enough but entirely abstruse nonetheless. I remember attending an advanced investment conference some years ago sponsored by the head of the actuarial science department at a leading Canadian university. We spent a whole afternoon in a stuffy classroom on a sweltering June day learning about stochastic volatility. I am commonsensical but unmathematical by training if not temperament and found the whole thing extremely tough slogging. I said as much to a fellow prisoner going down the elevator afterwards; the individual in question runs an enormous Canadian bond portfolio. He replied succinctly, "It is tough slogging." Incidentally, stochastic volatility, so far as I remember, is random volatility, in other words price variance that cannot otherwise be explained. In the Greek alphabet soup of financial science, random volatility is denoted by the letter zeta. You are consequently advised to keep Zeta the Greek far away from your portfolio.

While the mathematical linguistics of index portfolio management can appear difficult, the concepts are not, or at least they are not counterintuitive. The philosopher and mathematician Bertrand Russell once said that people are perfectly capable of using words intelligently without having the faintest idea what they mean. Take *coronary thrombosis*. I can readily use those words in a sentence because I know it means something like having a heart attack. But that's about the extent of it. It's the same with index investing buzz: derivatives, duration, optimization or whatever. Many people in the investment industry can use these words on a daily basis without really having any conceptual understanding of what they mean.

The good news for individual investors, however, is that all this really doesn't matter. Indexes, index products and index math are like Mount Everest: they're there. Consequently, ordinary investors don't need to worry about understanding the subtleties of index construction or how to run a regression analysis, determine the duration of a bond portfolio or price an index option. It is more commonsensical to try to understand the basic concepts and take the index universe as a given—let the professors deal with the rest.

On this last point, the combined subjects of index investing, index derivatives and their related quantitative underpinnings seem to attract the attention of professors manqué in the investment industry, individuals who like to speak in binomial equations but frequently don't in fact have statistical or mathematical academic backgrounds at all (I call these types "professors," with no disrespect intended to my professor who was long J.P. Morgan and Caterpillar, the world's most peculiar portfolio). By contrast, it has been my good fortune to meet some extremely impressive academics who have readily made the transition from university life to quantitative and index money management; many of them, by the way, are very good and patient teachers. In the end, the complexities of index investing should teach humility. Nonetheless, for those who prefer clarity to precision, read on; but I offer my apologies if I have offended any Ph.D. out there along the way.

INDEX INVESTING AND CAPITAL MARKETS THEORY 101

This book is about index investing, not modern portfolio theory. But it is interesting to consider how many of the concepts behind modern risk management, particularly in the context of managing a portfolio of stocks, derive from index principles and how they eloquently make the case for index investing.

Every investor knows or should know that while the variability of returns from individual stocks in a portfolio is important, the extent to which stocks move in tandem (this is termed covariance, the measure of the degree of parallelism between the returns of two different assets) is even more important. In a famous example, an investor on an imaginary island has only two investment choices: the local resort hotel or the local umbrella manufacturer. By investing exclusively in umbrellas, the investor will have a winning strategy only part of the time (i.e. during rainy season); but by investing equally in the two concerns, the investor benefits all of the time from the effects of seasonality which are after all responsible for the success of both ventures. By extension, setting up a stock portfolio composed exclusively of, say, consumer goods stocks or banks or cyclicals will ensure that—while you will see different price fluctuations for your investment at the end of the day—you won't have ensured any sort of portfolio diversification at all. Instead, the intelligent investor will diversify his/her holdings not just on the basis of having a willy-nilly collection of stocks, but by having broad representation from the various economic sectors that make up the overall equity market. This is called diversification and it just makes common sense.

But there's more to it than plain common sense. By spreading your bets through diversification, it can be mathematically demonstrated that an investor will reduce portfolio risk substantially (portfolio risk is usually defined by the contemporary investment industry as the standard deviation of returns, which measures in percentage terms the anticipated degree of price variability or volatility of a security or asset class). But not all risk. Stock prices themselves are variable, but a portfolio of stocks can also be risky because of general market volatility. This dichotomy is summed up neatly by the distinction between unsystematic (individual stock) and systematic (market) risk. As we have seen (Chapter 4), there is a handy "index" way to measure the risk of individual securities in a portfolio against the index itself, and that is called beta.

So portfolio diversification mitigates but does not entirely eliminate risk. This still presents a problem. If you mention the words "take on risk—maybe not a whole lot, but a bit" to anyone in his or her right mind, the reply should be, "What's in it for me?" Anyone who assumes risk should rationally expect to be compensated for so doing with a risk premium of some sort. Since diversification substantially reduces unsystematic risk, the risk the stock investor is left with is systematic or market risk. That's where the "compensation" factor has to come into play.

Thanks to the pioneering work of a number of quantitatively gifted academics (primarily Markowitz and Sharpe), it was found to be possible to create what are termed "efficient" portfolios that can provide the maximum level of return for each unit of risk an investor is willing to undertake. The most efficient portfolio of all, of course, is the market (i.e. the index return itself) since it provides the highest level of return with the correspondingly lowest level of risk. Consequently, if we can measure market risk by our base 100 index, consider the following outcomes and how investors should view their risk/reward accordingly:

1. 0/100 risk factor: the investor does not wish to take on any market risk preferring a guaranteed return instead (typical investor: the T-bill investor).
2. 50/100 risk factor: the investor wishes to take on some market risk (typical investor: the balanced fund investor).
3. 100/100 risk factor: the investor wishes to take on market risk (typical investor: the index investor).
4. 125/100 risk factor: the investor wishes to take on more than market risk (typical investor: the active fund investor).
5. 150/100 risk factor: the investor wishes to take on much more than market risk (typical investor: the aggressive fund investor).

The moral in all of this is that, if you want to take on portfolio risk that is 25% higher than the overall market, you'd better make sure you are getting compensated to do so. Otherwise, you're simply betting against the house. As we have seen, beating the overall market by 25% is a tricky enough proposition; to do so consistently over time, while not unheard of, is more than a trick. Nonetheless, this simple schematic illustrates on an easy-to-understand, comparative basis what you should be looking for in terms of a return requirement for taking on more than market risk (i.e. by investing in an actively managed stock fund). Index investors at least always know precisely what risk they are assuming and are assured of receiving an appropriate risk premium for so doing. And this is precisely how efficient portfolio investment is defined by modern portfolio theory.

INDEX FUND MATH

On a late June 1999 trading day, the Dow was up 1.50%, the S&P 500 was up 1.51% and the Nasdaq Composite was up 1.52%. One day in the market is just usually a statistical blip, but it is curious that these three very different indexes (see Chapter 2) should produce almost the same return pattern if only for a day. In fact, the leading equity market indexes—just like the individual securities that make up the indexes themselves—frequently move closely in tandem, particularly over time. This can be gauged by the statistical measure of covariance or parallelism as we have just seen. For example, while they can exhibit significant differences on a year-over-year basis, over longer time horizons (10 years) the huge Wilshire 5000 (which is really 7,400 names) and the select Dow 30 have diverged by less than one-half of one percentage point in terms of annualized performance. Less surprisingly, over the last 20 years the S&P 500's average annual performance was 13.6% versus the Wilshire 5000's 13.3% return. Similarly, the Toronto 35 has tracked the broader TSE 300 remarkably closely over time—remember that is only 35 stocks against a universe of 300.

Why this should be the case is a result of the way indexes are designed and of the impact that the largest market capitalization stocks have on overall index price movement. Index statisticians measure this "correlation" pattern through what is termed regression analysis, a complex subject well outside the scope of our look at index investing. But in simple terms, the relationship between a portfolio (or fund's) return and the index return can be defined by the closeness in fit (termed the R-squared and measured as a percentage like our friend beta) between the performance of the two. For instance, a fund with an R-squared of .80 (the index again being 1.00) can attribute the preponderance of its performance to the market itself, with only a small portion attributable to the manager's skill or strategy in running the fund. A fund with an R-squared of .95 basically reflects the index return itself (funds so managed are called "closet index" funds; see the chart in Chapter 1). The point is that portfolios have an easily measurable return relationship with the major indexes and, particularly in the case of capitalization weighted indexes, a surprisingly small number of large stocks can closely mimic the overall index return.

Consequently, index funds can be managed by means of several techniques that are based on the foregoing index math concepts. But just before we begin, remember the comment made previously that it is naïve to think that even index funds are entirely what they seem, i.e. a portfolio of precisely the same stocks as are represented in the index itself. It is also important to note that not all of these techniques would be applied to the management of the same index fund:

1. Index replication: The fund holds precisely the same stocks in the same proportion or weightings as they appear in the index. Note,

however, that the return to the investor is net of management fees and some slippage, i.e. less than the pure index return (see discussion of MERs and tracking error, Chapter 1). While most pure index funds employ a full replication portfolio management strategy, some do not (particularly when they track fairly illiquid indexes or are "passive plus" funds; such funds generally employ "sampling" to get around this, see below).

2. Portfolio optimization: Largely used for bond indexing, portfolio optimization permits the index fund to hold a smaller number of securities than the index itself. This makes sense for a bond index portfolio because of the known and reasonably predictable mathematical relationships between bonds of various terms to maturity and credit quality; in addition, many bonds in a bond index are simply unavailable for purchase since they are locked up in institutional accounts. Where optimization is used for equity portfolios, the so-called "optimized" portfolio is designed to have a high R-squared or "tight fit" with the index itself by ensuring that the fund holds a statistically viable percentage of the total market capitalization of the index. What makes optimization feasible is that, over the longer term, mathematical modeling can ensure that the absence of some index stocks from the fund portfolio is statistically relatively insignificant although tracking error is still a real risk over the short term.

3. Sampling: This technique is usually liquidity driven and employed with both stock and bond index portfolios. For example, the illiquidity or even availability of certain securities often makes it difficult to replicate an index cost-effectively. So instead of trying, the manager will use sampling techniques to create a representative subset of securities selected in proportion to their index weightings which also matches key index characteristics such as

industry groupings, market capitalization, dividend yield and so on. For example, Vanguard's Wilshire 5,000 or Total Market fund currently owns approximately 3,100 names out of a potential universe of about 7,400, i.e. far less than half. Similarly, index funds tracking the Lehman Bond Index employ sampling because of the large number of illiquid fixed-income securities in this enormous index.

4. Tracking error: As we have seen, there is usually always a difference between an index's return and an index portfolio's (or fund's) return. With new index funds, wider tracking error may occur in the short term and then narrow over time as the fund grows in size. Although bigger is usually better when it comes to indexing, this does not mean that the gap can ever be completely eliminated, primarily due to the various costs that index funds incur. Again, the higher the management fee and other administrative expenses (e.g. brokerage commissions and custodial fees), the higher the tracking error.

5. Rebalancing: To ensure that index portfolios track their respective indexes closely, the index manager must continuously monitor and occasionally "rebalance" the portfolio as circumstances warrant. Rebalancing is also required to account for changes in the stocks and bonds in the relevant index, handle reinvested income (i.e. dividends and interest earned by the fund) and manage cash coming into or going out of the fund (i.e. unitholder purchases and redemptions).

The New Index Math

So far, readers could be forgiven for thinking that passively managed or index funds employ an objective form of stock selection methodology based on the composition of the index pure and simple. In fact, the management of index funds (particularly structured index funds) can entail a degree of subjectivity in terms of the stock selection process (see Chapter 6 for more on how passive managers can outperform the index and comments about structured index funds). Generally, index fund managers can get away with this because of the dependability of proprietary, quantitative optimization models that have been developed by academics and the Street itself. Established indexes such as the S&P 500 are comprised of companies chosen by committees using strict rules and selection criteria, which are well known to the investment and academic communities. Consequently, statistical index profiles can be created which permit a kind of "active/passive" security selection process that will nonetheless deliver the index return within a few basis points. On the other hand, as and when we see Internet index funds (see Chapter 2), their managers may not wish to indulge in the new math with their funds because of the high degree of subjectivity, turnover and volatility implicit with the newer indexes.

Index Investing Math

Despite the seeming complexity of all of the foregoing, investors in index mutual funds really only need to know one number that impacts their investment performance: that is NAV or Net Asset Value. NAV is the way in which a fund computes the value of its assets (usually daily) by totaling the market value of all securities owned less any liabilities; the balance is divided by the number of shares or units outstanding. The resulting figure is termed the net asset value per share and index fund NAVs are published daily in the financial media. For index participation unitholders, pricing is continuous during trading hours on the floor of the exchange and, as always with traded securities, subject to a bid/ask spread.

INDEX DERIVATIVE MATH

"Derivatives" may be one of the most overused, misunderstood and feared words in the lexicon of the financial world today. Like a rogue elephant tromping through a jungle village, derivatives have—according to the popular headlines—been responsible for gargantuan losses at Fortune 500 corporations, the near bankruptcy of Orange County, California and the demise of Barings, the venerable 233-year old British investment bank, through overleveraged index trading concurrently on the Hong Kong, Singapore and U.S. derivative exchanges. Either derivatives need a good PR agent or there's less here than meets the eye.

We have seen the conventional definition of derivatives before: derivatives are financial instruments that derive their value from something else, e.g. stock index futures from a stock index, currency options from the spot foreign exchange market, etc., etc. Derivatives *derive*. As far as definitions go, that's fine up to a point. But it's like saying that the sun shines: true, but not terribly meaningful.

There is a better way of looking at this:

1. Derivatives can help identify, delineate or unbundle and in turn manage virtually every kind of financial and business risk we can imagine. In the context of index investing, the primary risk is the market's systematic risk, which for the first time (short of never owning stocks at all) can be segregated and effectively managed through index options and futures.
2. Just about every type of risk—once unbundled—can be priced. Risk is priced by the market itself, by market volatility, by its relationship to an underlying security or the index portfolio from which it derives its value and also in relation to changes in the level of interest rates.

3. Once priced, risk can be traded. There are natural buyers and sellers of each aspect of the risk that derivatives define and price in the marketplace. For example, purchasing index options provides investors with the opportunity to buy market participation or market insurance at limited downside risk. Selling index options permits investors to capture volatility or market risk on a leveraged basis. Buying index futures produces leveraged exposure to the market, while selling futures against an equity portfolio is a form of insurance protection. Investors can also combine the purchase and sale of options and/or futures on the same underlying index to produce a range of risk-neutral strategies. There is usually always a natural buyer and seller for the same index risk profile through the derivative market.

4. The leverage feature of index options and futures also means that investors can increase their potential returns from index investing by assuming certain predetermined degrees of risk. This is relatively efficient from a risk/return perspective. For example, an index option buyer cannot lose more than the premium paid for the contract since the right to buy or sell the underlying index at a specific price is valid only up until the expiration date. In addition to these conventional strategies, index derivatives offer investors possibilities for market participation, hedging or creating risk-neutral strategies that are limited virtually only by their imaginations.

5. Despite their seeming complexity and the proliferation of products in the marketplace today, index derivatives come in just two basic forms. By understanding how the pricing of the two instruments differs, investors can gain a better understanding of how to trade them and how the market works. While

oversimplified, index futures are priced on the basis of current interest rates, while index options are priced on the basis of volatility.

6. Index futures are priced largely though not exclusively on the basis of the current index level plus the prevailing level of short-term interest rates. In common with forward rate agreements, swaps and other comparable derivative products, index futures pricing basically reflects the time value of money. An equity index futures contract combines the price of the current value of the stocks in the index along with the cost of carry (the short-term interest cost) required to finance the equivalent stock position until the contract expires. But the theoretical price of owning all the stocks in an index will always differ from the price of a futures contract not only because of a) short-term interest rates but also b) dividends. Since index futures don't pay dividends, an adjustment for the "fair value" of the futures contract must be made by adding in the cost of borrowing and subtracting the regular dividend stream. Things becomes a bit more complicated than that as the futures "basis" (or cost of carry) has a life of its own and is consequently itself subject to volatility. But the basic formula is: cash market index price today + short-term interest rate – index dividends X term to maturity = current index futures price.

7. Index options are priced on the basis of volatility. While there are other key components in option pricing formulas, index options are largely priced on the basis of volatility—in other words, the risk or probability of potential price variability in the underlying index. The time value of money is a fairly straightforward concept. Volatility is not. The option pricing formula takes

into account the market price of the index, the current cost of money or short-term interest rate, the time to expiry of the contract, dividend flows and the historical volatility (usually a fairly short-term moving average) of the underlying index. By combining all these variables, the model produces a price called the option premium which becomes the cost of index participation or market insurance.

8. While the business of derivatives is managing and benefiting from market risk, derivative markets themselves offer a high degree of stability and efficiency. The standardization of exchange-traded derivative contracts ensures orderly, efficient and liquid markets. A futures contract is standardized so that the creditworthiness of the counterparty (the other side of the trade) is assured by the clearing corporation, and market integrity is maintained through the discipline of margin and the daily marking to market of all positions. Similarly, index option contracts are guaranteed by the clearing corporation so that, in effect, it stands as purchaser for every contract sold and seller for every contract purchased. Derivative markets are also highly visible and extremely liquid (at least in the U.S.).

9. Since their introduction in the early 1980s, index options and futures have given investors a great deal of flexibility in managing their portfolios. As previously noted, institutional interest in derivatives was originally cost driven because of transactional ease and high degree of liquidity; retail investor interest was initially performance and leverage driven. But what individual investors have learned about the performance attributes of derivatives has now become a main focus of institutional participation in the index derivative market.

HOW INDEX ARBITRAGE WORKS

We've frequently alluded to index arbitrage, the pricing relationship between the index basket of stocks and its corresponding index futures contract. In a theoretically priced world, there should be equilibrium between the two; in the real world, frequently there is not. If an investor borrows at 5.5% to finance an index basket of stocks which has a dividend yield of 1.75%, then the investor's cost of carry (i.e. effective cost of financing the position) would be 3.75%. In theory then, the fair value of the corresponding futures contract would be the current index base level plus 3.75% annualized. This is termed the futures basis as we have seen. Frequently, however, mispricings arise that are at variance with what the theoretical basis would normally be indicated to be. These may be a result of many factors, including the actual choice of the interest rate used in the fair value calculation, the bid/ask spread for the basket of index stocks and the calculation of the dividend yield itself (which is actually calculated as the present value of the dividend stream for futures pricing purposes).

Net result regardless of the cause: the futures basis can either end up being cheaper or richer than it should be in theory. Note however, that this mispricing is yield based and has nothing to do with the index or market return per se. What it does do is give rise to arbitrage opportunities for professional and institutional traders. For example, if futures are trading at a discount of so many basis points to fair value, the amount of that discount represents the pick-up an index fund can add to its portfolio return if it sells its stock portfolio and buys a combination of T-bills and index futures contracts. Because the futures contract will converge with the cash market price at expiry, the synthetic index portfolio will achieve the same return as would be the case with the basket of stocks, but plus the sweetener resulting from the futures mispricing. This is called an index swap trade.

Arbitrageurs—either index fund managers or pro traders—can pick off such discrepancies to add value to their portfolio holdings as we have seen (Chapter 6); in addition to the extra liquidity these trades add to the overall market, they also help ensure that the futures market and the cash market don't trade out of sync for long.

MORE ON HOW INDEX OPTIONS ARE PRICED

Since most individual investors may try index options at some point, I thought a little more 101 was in order. Option pricing is probably the most difficult bit of math an index investor will encounter. The curious should consult the experts. The best book on options is still Lawrence McMillan's *Options as a Strategic Investment*; for more information on index derivatives generally, consult the various exchange websites.

The key point to understand about index options and futures for that matter is that, unlike their corresponding underlying securities, they do not exist until someone wants to trade them. Hence an index option contract is created when a trade is executed between a buyer and seller for a specific contract. Pricing for index options is therefore dynamic, based not just on the market price of the underlying index but also on its current volatility and other factors.

The original option pricing model, the Black-Scholes model dating from 1973, has been updated and modified by several subsequent models. Option pricing is complex, and price analysis depends not just on the market premium quoted on the floor of the exchange but also on its "fair value," a process comparable to that undertaken by an analyst who seeks to analyze the fair value of a stock. There are five principal factors which affect the premium level of an option:

1. The price of the underlying stock or index relative to the strike price of the option.
2. Time until expiration.
3. Dividends.
4. Interest rates.
5. Volatility.

Underlying Index Price and Strike Price

The difference between the underlying index price and the option strike price is a major determinant of the premium of an option. The amount that an option is in the money, or more specifically the difference between the underlying index price and the strike price for an in-the-money option, is referred to as the option's intrinsic value. Only in-the-money index options have intrinsic value. An at-the-money or out-of-the-money index option has no intrinsic value because there is no benefit to exercising the option. Note that virtually all index derivative contracts are now cash-settled, which means that the contract holder either receives or pays the difference between the purchase or sale value of the contract in cash at expiration rather than taking delivery of the underlying index securities.

Time Value

Generally, the longer the time remaining until an index option's expiration, the higher the option's time value. Time value is a portion of an option's premium not accounted for by intrinsic value or other factors. With all other variables constant, option premium will decline— or "decay"—as the time to expiration becomes shorter. Time decay does not occur at a constant rate, but increases exponentially as the time to expiration shortens. At this point, index options lose value very quickly until they expire worthless (assuming no intrinsic value).

Dividends

Dividends affect the value of an index option through their impact on the price of the underlying index shares. Dividends are also the "guaranteed" component of return from equity investment, hence the higher the dividend, the more secure the return. Generally, on the ex-dividend date, the value of a stock will decline precisely by the amount of the declared dividend. This will obviously affect the pricing of the index option contract. In stock option pricing, high cash dividends tend to imply lower call premiums and higher put premiums and vice versa.

Interest Rates

Interest rates are a key part of the options pricing model, because they provide the risk-free rate (T-bill rate) against which all investment returns are contrasted. As a general rule, higher interest rates tend to result in higher call premiums and lower put premiums and vice versa.

Volatility

As we have seen, volatility is the key mathematical measure of a stock's or index's price variability. Volatility is generally measured by the standard deviation of returns. Securities with wide price swings are said to have high volatility, while securities whose price remains fairly stable exhibit low volatility. But volatility does not mean market direction (as in "the market is volatile" means that the market is going down); rather it is a measure of price swings (chop) and consequently capital uncertainty. It is also interesting but true that as stock market values increase, volatility can also decrease. For example, if a stock trades at $50, quickly rises to $100, then moves down to $70 and settles at $80, the average price change becomes more constant as it decreases in percentage terms.

In the options market, high historical volatility has the effect of directly increasing premiums and consequently is the key measure to watch in trading these products. Option software package conveniently analyzes fair option premium value and market value; some traders simply try to arbitrage the difference between the two. In a kind of mirror image, implied volatility is the volatility measure of the underlying security as reflected by the current option premium itself. The next step is seeing how price movements between the underlying and the index option contract track.

Delta–Key Risk Management Measure

That is the job of delta. Delta is the option pricing algorithm that measures the expected change in the option premium level for any given change in the price of the underlying index. If an index options trader understands nothing else, this would have to be it. In simple terms, delta measures the probability that an index option will expire in the money and it involves the other option pricing variables we have just considered in this process. For instance, with an at-the-money index option, delta is generally .50, which indicates a 50/50 chance that the option will expire worthless (back to our index 100 idea again). If the underlying index increases in value, the (call) option premium will also increase and vice versa.

It is for this reason that delta is never a constant, but changes in response to movements in the price of the underlying index stocks. As an index call moves farther into the money, its delta will rise as it begins to lose its leverage potential and starts to behave more like the underlying index. Underlying price movement, however, isn't the only influence on delta. Changes in index volatility also have a significant impact on delta, as does the impact of time decay as the option moves towards expiration.

The highest delta for an option is always 1.00, meaning that it is in the money at expiration, and its price behaviour now precisely mirrors that of the underlying index; as such it now lacks any time value or leverage potential. If an option ends up at the money or out of the money at expiry, its delta sinks to zero, reflecting absolute insensitivity to any price changes in the underlying index.

The CBOE's VIX Index

Another index to the rescue. The Chicago Board Options Exchange Volatility Index (VIX) is a key volatility measure employed by traders and market pros. The index is a composite that computes the volatility of four nearby month OEX (S&P 100) option contracts (puts and calls) both in and just out of the money, thus providing a leading indicator of potential overall market variability.

CHAPTER 6

The Sophisticated
Indexer

———

IF YOU HAVE PERSEVERED THIS FAR, chances are you should now be convinced that index investment products are the only appropriate vehicles for implementing your personal asset allocation strategy (see further Chapter 7). What's more, you'll have come to the conclusion that it is pointless trying to beat the various market bogeys, being content to have your portfolio match them instead. Also think of all the money you'll save by no longer enriching those cigar smoking, red braces-wearing active fund managers who are paid far too much anyway. And you'll be guaranteed to sleep better, worry less, live longer, be happier, etc., etc., too.

But now to confound matters, we are going to see how active asset management principles can be applied to passive portfolios—in other words, how passive can become active. We'll also see how you can actually take an index apart and put it back together again and look at some forms of deconstructed index products.

Confused? Don't be. Let's return to some basic principles as to what an index is in the first place, only this time from a slightly different perspective. Indexes are composed of stocks that have a number of things in common: a certain size of market capitalization, varied industry representation, strong financials, liquidity and other inclusion criteria. But indexes still consist of individual securities that have special characteristics of their own. Take the common investment management dichotomy between growth and value "style" investors. There are a couple of distinctively growth and/or value indexes out there, such as the S&P BARRA Growth and Value Indexes, and there is a small number of highly specialized index funds in the U.S. that are designed to mimic a pure growth or value style. But most index funds are classified as blended portfolios, because most indexes consist of both value and growth stocks, although because of their price or market cap structures, one style can be dominant over the other.

Indexes also consist of industry sectors. The sophisticated indexer can deconstruct the index by sector as well as by style, and in fact the sector approach can offer the most value-added performance potential. There are also new wrinkles that involve cherry picking existing indexes to create new concept indexes, such as ethical index funds as we shall see.

Finally, there is the whole realm of active management of a passive fund. A variety of techniques designed to add value and minimize tracking error enable passive fund managers to beat their respective indexes. Nobody said the index investing revolution was going to be straightforward or dull, especially not for sophisticated indexers.

HUGGING YOUR INDEX

If you're going to use an index as your equity proxy, you're going to want to be sure you are able to hug it, style and all.

But before we can truly become index huggers, let's go back in time once again to get our bearings. As the U.S. equity market boomed in the late 1960s and early 1970s (see Chapter 4), market leadership was firmly in the hands of 50 or so very large capitalization stocks that represented the best and brightest of American industry. They were called the Nifty Fifty, the "can-do-no-wrong," go-go growth stocks that had become a one-decision investment for institutional investors despite their extremely high valuations. Many of these names are very familiar and still with us today: IBM, Xerox, Kodak, Polaroid, McDonald's, Disney, etc. But in 1972, just before the onslaught of the great bear market of the mid-70s, these stocks were trading at P/E multiples averaging between 80-90X earnings. Needless to say, when the market cracked as a result of the 1973 oil embargo and other global economic forces, the Nifty Fifty were shot down from the sky and U.S. institutional investors questioned what they had ever really liked about large-cap growth stocks in the first place. Don't forget that stocks were not yet as mainstream in institutional portfolios then as they are now.

Strangely reminiscent of the Nifty Fifty era of the 1970s, although not at the same extreme valuations levels, the S&P 500 has become not only the dominant U.S. equity benchmark but also a magnet for investors, and is viewed as a safe haven in a volatile market environment almost, though not quite, like the U.S. treasury (bond) market. But as we have seen, the S&P 500 isn't a particularly broad measure of market performance; the same is equally true of the big-cap Toronto 35 Index. Since they are both weighted by market capitalization, the largest stocks in the index have the most clout. That means an S&P 500 index investor is really getting in bed with a select group of big-cap growth stocks. Even Vanguard's Bogle feels compelled to remind investors that the S&P 500 isn't "the market."

Consider the corporate giants that make up the top ten S&P 500 names along with their approximate respective percentages of the total index market cap (just under 22% of the entire S&P 500 at time of writing):

Microsoft (ticker: MSFT: Nasdaq):	4.02%
General Electric (GE: NYSE):	3.45%
Wal-Mart (WMT: NYSE):	2.01%
Merck (MRK: NYSE):	1.93%
Intel (INTC: Nasdaq):	1.87%
Pfizer PFE: NYSE):	1.72%
Exxon (XON: NYSE):	1.67%
AT&T (T: NYSE):	1.66%
MCI WorldCom (WCOM: Nasdaq):	1.58%
Coca-Cola (KO: NYSE):	1.57%

These stocks have a disproportionate impact on the S&P 500 Index and their dominance is self-sustained by, among other forces, index funds themselves. Remember that for every new dollar coming into an index fund, 1.87 cents of that must automatically be committed to purchasing Intel. These stocks have also not been cheap to own. The composite S&P 500 P/E multiple has been in the high 20s for quite some time (another memorable period in the last 15 years when this was also true: the summer of 1987), but the P/E ratio for many of the top index stocks has been much higher, over 50 times trailing earnings, which is where the Nifty Fifty echo began among those on the Street with long memories.

Nonetheless, you can't argue with success. The S&P 500 has been the place to be over the past number of years sporting a 30% average annual return. Even the infamous hedge fund Long Term Capital, managed by Nobel laureates who helped create the option pricing model and define modern risk management, but which nonetheless took enormous, highly leveraged market bets and almost brought the global financial house falling down, returned on average only about 18% annually to investors, far less than the S&P and right off the map on any sort of risk-adjusted basis. But it has been argued by some analysts that investors, seeing the outsized returns from the largest cap stocks, may have been tempted to abandon the overriding principle of prudent diversification and target their portfolios towards an ever-narrowing slice of the equity market pie. As proof, they cite the fact that in 1994 the top 50 stocks in the S&P 500 accounted for about 45% of the index's total market capitalization. Today, that number is approximately 56%. On the other hand, similar concerns about the narrowness and/or high valuation of the S&P 500 in 1994 would have cost investors hundreds of index points of return if they had stayed away because of them.

Given its extraordinary degree of liquidity and investor popularity, the S&P 500's success itself has been a self-fulfilling factor, since portfolio managers don't get paid for loading up on small-cap stocks that are going to revolutionize the world in five years if the action today is in the big-cap issues. There's also the momentum argument to consider: investors are prepared to pay up for performance and the index names have delivered. No one can deny the earnings performance of a Microsoft, the global strategy performance of an MCI or the dramatic corporate repositioning performance of even a stodgy old AT&T. Then there's the fact of market rotation. The same industry groups in a highly diversified index like the S&P 500 don't always outperform each and every year; more typically, some of last year's winners are this year's laggards and vice versa.

There are just two final points to be made about the appropriateness of an index such as the S&P 500 for every investor. The first is a generic index fund benefit. Active managers and/or investors have to figure out what's what in terms of the underlying fundamentals, and then decide who's the next comer and who's not. Financials? Cyclicals? Tech? Index investors at least have the benefit of exposure at all times to all major sectors, which is at least a form of insurance policy for not missing the party if not a guarantee of significant portfolio outperformance. But there is also life beyond the S&P 500. Which brings us to the second point about hugging your index, and while it's an obvious one, it is perhaps still worth mentioning: make sure that the index you are hugging is the right one. Obviously, there can be many different kinds of index investor either through funds or SPDRs or their equivalents where they exist: large-cap index investors via the S&P 500, mid-cap investors via the S&P 400, small cap via the Russell 2000 or S&P 600, value via the BARRA Value Index, Internet via the whatever index one day soon, etc., etc. Consequently, the index benchmark that is appropriate for you isn't necessarily the S&P 500 (see Chapter 2 for more non-S&P 500 options) or any other one index.

So while index investing may be a one-stop investment decision , it's not a no-brainer. We have seen the problems with the TSE 300 and tried to outline the characteristics of the leading North American indexes in Chapter 2. Each has different attributes, each has different structural qualities, each has different performance proclivities. Consequently, it's a fault to think that one index such as the S&P 500 is the final answer. It's not, but it can be part of the answer. So caveat index investor.

HOW INDEXERS OUTPERFORM THE INDEX

Sophisticated investors give careful consideration to the nature of the index in which they are investing; some have even figured out how to make the index work over time on their behalf. One way is by beating the index. Asserting that an indexer can beat the index should at first blush appear to be something of an oxymoron. But it can happen and it does. The technique is called "passive plus" management, and while the incremental returns generated by these programs tend to be minuscule (measured in basis points or 1/100s of one percentage point), on a billion dollar plus portfolio, they can add up. With a passive plus management style, it is possible to actively run an index fund that will outperform its nominal index benchmark. There are several recognized ways for a passive fund manager to do this:

1. Figure out how to trade around the regular (typically annual though often more frequent) index revisions which of course involve the inclusion and deletion of various stocks. In the U.S. in particular, there is always plenty of speculation as to what stocks are coming in and what's going out, so astute trading around these (frequently predictable) events can add value to the index portfolio. This is not to say that this is not lacking an element of speculation, but hey, index managers need something to do to keep from falling asleep at their desks.

2. Pick your spots in the index. Indexers who are running optimized portfolios will consciously overweight certain index sectors for a variety of reasons (this is termed "tilting" and is intended to add if not enormous at least incremental return to the portfolio). For example, the manager's call could be based on market capitalization (e.g. overweighting mid-cap stocks), potential sector outperformance (e.g. overweighting the banks in a declining interest rate environment) or, horror of horrors, the outlook for selected individual equities to outperform based on changes in earnings estimates or what have you. The magic of

index math enables the passive manager to track the index return within a few basis points, which gives the 25-year old rocket
scientists employed by his/her firm something to do by con-
stantly reviewing and trading the index constituent stocks in
an attempt to add value to the portfolio.

3. Hold higher yielding fixed-income securities as your good faith
   margin for index futures positions or simply as your cash allocation. So-called "synthetic" index portfolios are usually comprised of T-bills and index futures contracts. As we have seen,
   many index mutual funds are run along these derivative lines. Any
   futures position requires a small amount of cash down (termed
   good faith margin) and is marked to market daily, which means
   that funds are credited to or debited from your account depending on where the market moves vis-à-vis your position. The most
   commonly used form of margin is 3-month T-bills; however, other
   fixed-income securities are permissible. If you substituted higher-
   yielding, short-term government bonds for T-bills, the difference
   accrues to the fund's bottom line but also implies the assumption
   of considerably more capital risk.

4. Some passive funds actually hold index participation units and
   cash exclusively instead of the constituent index stocks. This is extremely cost-effective because the cost of rebalancing the index
   portfolio is effectively borne by the trust that creates the index
   participation units, not the fund manager. In this case, a penny
   saved is a penny earned. Just think of the gall or marketing genius,
   depending on your point of view, implicit in this. I know of at least
   one Toronto 35 index fund that purchases nothing but TIPS 35
   units for 0.05% and then resells them to the consumer in an
   Toronto 35 index fund package with an MER of well over 2%.
   Talk about a gross-up.

5. "Arb" the cash and futures market. In the discussion of program trading and arbitrage (Chapter 4), we saw how index arbitrage creates risk-free incremental returns. Managers of synthetic index portfolios will try to exploit any anomalies between the cash market and the futures to add value, ie. by buying cheap index futures and shorting the index basket of stocks or shorting expensive futures and going long the index basket. The more the manager is able to do this, the more incremental return he/she can add to the index portfolio. Curiously, of all the value-added index strategies considered here, this is the least risky since it involves no credit or security selection risk per se.

6. Undertake fee-based securities lending arrangements with natural borrowers of securities (i.e. short-sellers and derivative traders), see further p. 82. Facilitated by trust companies, custodians and other so-called "securities processors," securities lending (in which stocks are "borrowed" for short sales over certain periods of time) can add tiny but helpful amounts of incremental return to an index fund portfolio.

These techniques have given rise to a range of computer-driven index management strategies that are designed to outperform the index return (see Structured Index Funds on p. 141). While the institutional investment community is comfortable with the idea of benchmarking equity assets (i.e. employing index fund management) and then immediately turning around and trying to beat the bogey, the concept is much less familiar to the individual investor. Perhaps the point is that passive plus management has been practised by institutional investors for quite some time, in part in the spirit of building a better mouse trap and in part because performance is what the institutional community is fixated on; after all, that's how they get paid.

Since many existing index funds are managed on an optimized basis and some are consciously managed to try to beat the benchmark, the intelligent investor may well wonder if the arguments that have been made in favour of indexing thus far don't contain an element of sham. Point taken, but after all indexing, like all investing, is ultimately a matter of definition.

DECONSTRUCTING THE INDEX

Implicit in active fund management theory is the notion that some investors know more than the market. Indexers are not necessarily immune from this fallacy (if they are wrong) or blinding truth (if they are right), and by understanding that indexes are made up of industry sectors, they can actually do something about it.

We have seen that the TSE 300 comprises 14 industry groups or sectors, which in turn form the sub-indexes of the Toronto market; the new S&P/TSE 60 has 11, which perform the same function. In the U.S., the biggies such as the Dow, S&P 500 and so on have been further broken down such that there are now approximately 60 different sector indexes that track the performance of the different industry groups. Major industries currently covered by sector indexes include companies in: banking, biotech, chemicals, drugs, environmental, consumer-related products, cyclicals, the oils, the airlines, telecommunications, insurance, gaming and now the Internet and e-commerce. By studying these indexes, and in particular focusing on the better performing sub-indexes, investors can gain insight as to the direction of the overall market and can try to achieve above-average (i.e. above index) returns by creating portfolios based on a basket of sector index stocks.

To make life easy for everybody, the Amex (sponsor of SPDRs—for full details about what they are, how they are traded and so on, see pp. 67 ff.) has recently created nine sector SPDRs covering: basic industries (ticker: XLB), consumer services (ticker: XLV), consumer staples (ticker: XLP), cyclicals/transportation (ticker: XLY), energy (ticker: XLE), financials (ticker: XLF), industrials (ticker: XLI), technology (ticker: XLK) and utilities (ticker: XLU). Not unsurprisingly, the technology SPDR has been the most popular (i.e. heavily traded) with investors to date. Trading in some of the other sector SPDRs is much less liquid, and there are no long-term performance numbers to look at as yet.

The beauty of sector SPDRs is that they enable investors to diversify their index portfolios away from the S&P 500. This is less paradoxical than it seems, because the S&P is heavily weighted with big-cap growth stocks and has been widely criticized by various commentators as to how truly representative it is of the overall U.S. equity market (see above). With the advent of sector SPDRs, a model U.S. index portfolio could include a 50% allocation to a major index such as the S&P 500 with the rest allocated to sector funds based on the investor's overall market call (see Core and Explore, p. 180). Index purists may object, but maintaining a passive core portfolio as well as rotating on an active/passive basis among the various sectors can almost certainly be guaranteed to beat the S&P 500 return. The problem, of course, is ensuring that the investor gets his/her sector allocation weightings right, the essential problem of all active management.

In a related development that is obviously designed to capitalize on the popularity of sector SPDRs, Barclays Global Investors has just announced its exhaustive list of new sector index products that are soon to be listed on the Amex and will expand investors' index trading options even further. As an aside, for a small exchange, the Amex has certainly acquired a track record for being big on innovation. Currently, the Amex lineup consists of SPDRs, the Nasdaq 100 Index Tracking Stock (ticker: QQQ), MidCap SPDRs (ticker: MDY), Diamonds (ticker: DIA), which track the Dow, 17 country WEBS (World Equity Benchmark Shares) and the nine U.S. market sector SPDRs. If anyone wanted to be innovative in Canada, perhaps sector index product development around the 11 groups in the S&P/TSE 60 could be undertaken on a similar basis to sector SPDRs.

Trading Notes

Sector SPDRs represent the same great deal as the overall S&P 500 index product, with an MER equivalent of 0.18% and relatively good liquidity. They don't seem to have caught on with the retail investing public as much as SPDRs, but that's not unexpected given their specialized nature. Unlike their sector mutual fund counterparts (see below), sector SPDRs may be bought on margin and sold short; also don't forget that they do pay dividends. Sector SPDRs also open up a range of new investment opportunities, including sector arbitrage (i.e. go long a basket of sector SPDRs if you think they're going to outperform and short basic SPDRs to cover your ass). Also remember that trading these products requires a brokerage account and of course your friendly broker is looking for his/her commission.

U.S. Sector Indexes

U.S. pro traders and institutional investors make use of a number of highly specialized sub-indexes to track key industry sectors and trade in and around the broader market.

Healthcare

- Amex Biotechnology Index (ticker: BTX)

- Amex Pharmaceutical Index (ticker: DRG)
- S&P Healthcare Index (ticker: HCX)

High Tech and Internet

- CBOE Software Index (ticker: CWX)
- Amex Inter@ctive Index (ticker: IIX)
- CBOE Internet Index (ticker: INX)
- Morgan Stanley High Tech Index (ticker: MSH)
- Philadelphia Semiconductor Index (ticker: SOX)
- CBOE Technology Index (ticker: TXX)
- Amex Computer Technology Index (ticker: XCI)

Transportation

- Philadelphia Airline Index (ticker: PLN)
- Amex Airline Index (ticker: XAL)
- S&P Transportation Index (ticker: TRX)

Telecommunications

- Philadelphia Phone Index (ticker: PNX)
- Amex N.A. Telecom Index (ticker: XTC)

Financial

- Philadelphia Stock Exchange/KBW Bank Index (ticker: BKX)
- American Stock Exchange Broker/Dealer Index (ticker: XBD)

Miscellaneous

- Morgan Stanley Cyclical Index (ticker: CYC)
- Morgan Stanley Consumer Index (ticker: CMR)
- CBOE Gaming Index (ticker: GAX)
- S&P Retail Index (ticker: RLX)

- Philadelphia Stock Exchange Oil Service Index (ticker: OSX)
- New York Stock Exchange Unweighted Average.

Sector Funds

For sector players, the new sector SPDRs offer an interesting alternative to sector mutual funds, and in particular Fidelity's popular Select family of industry sector funds, which were previously the only game in town.

Both sector SPDRs and actively managed sector funds permit investors to indulge in sector rotation with the basic objective of beating the overall market. While sector funds aren't really index funds per se, they are reasonably representative of their respective sector sub-indexes. Another good reason for considering sector products is that they can be good vehicles for investors focused on sector rotation rather than pure market timing, which carried to its extreme is the more aggressive strategy of being either fully invested or 100% in cash.

In the U.S. market, Fidelity currently offers 40 sector funds in all, covering everything from financial services to health care and technology, with subsets including more specialized groups such as insurance, PC makers, telecom equipment manufacturers, etc. It's really quite an impressive array. There are even at least two independent tracking/advisory services that make buy and sell recommendations based on their outlook for the various Fidelity sector funds (for a fee) of which I am aware.

Another newer player in the U.S. sector funds market is Rydex. There are currently 14 Rydex sector funds covering Biotech, Electronics, Banking, Leisure, Energy, Retail, Tech and so on; five Rydex funds beat their Fidelity counterparts, two by a wide margin, last year.

Canadian investors currently have the choice of five Fidelity Focus Funds sponsored by Fidelity Investments Canada and sold by brokers and financial planners. C.I. also offers similar sector funds. Altamira has launched an innovative e-commerce fund which has done well and seems to be on the verge of introducing more sector funds. CIBC has a Canadian financial services sector fund and so on. AIC Advantage, which has concentrated holdings in the financial services industry, including mutual fund companies (proving the theorem that there is usually more money to be made in holding the stock of fund companies than the funds they sponsor), has been categorized as a sector fund and then de-categorized again as a general equity fund. The line can readily blur between what is mainline equity and what is in fact a sector fund.

The biggest splash to date has been caused by the five Fidelity funds, which are: Financial Services, Technology, Health Care, Consumer Products and Natural Resources. Since their inception in June 1997, Canadian investors would have been able to handily beat the S&P 500 by holding four of the Fidelity sector funds (exception: Natural Resources), although we're back on the same old turf regarding active fund MERs and loads (see pros and cons of each approach, pp. 61 ff.).

In common with all active management practice, successful sector fund investors must do their homework by:

1. Diligently researching each industry sector before investing. You not only have to know what your industry is doing, but may also want to check broader market, business and economic trends as well. Know what the leading sector analysts are saying, and understand not just what the industry's past performance has been, but what it's likely to do in future.

2. Researching the range of individual sector funds. Different sector funds even covering the same industry employ widely varying strategies and portfolio structures. In terms of comparative

performance, compare apples with apples (example: the representative benchmark for a utility sector fund would be the Dow Jones Utility Average rather than the broader Dow 30).

3. Considering factors besides fund performance and fees. Research capability and commitment are key. Also try to watch how much trading's going on. High portfolio turnover not only undermines good performance, it can also create an unwelcome tax liability for unitholders.

4. Placing your industry or sector knowledge in context. Despite the fact that some sectors, such as e-commerce or the Internet, may not currently be making any profits, they can still have good/great/stupendous long-term growth potential. Also beware of making decisions based on isolated facts or an incomplete understanding of financial, operational or industry data.

5. Buying what you know, as Warren Buffett succinctly put it. Sector funds can be especially useful for individuals with a close involvement with a particular industry. Otherwise, do your homework and make sure that your knowledge applies to the industry as a whole, not just to a particular company.

Paradoxically, especially given the theme of this book, there could be merit in considering an active manager if you want to pursue a deconstructed index or sector strategy. That's because, while loads and MERs are still vitally important, success with the sector approach is fundamentally a question of in-depth industry research. In addition, sector specialists frequently have a better sense of their stocks than active managers who must oversee a broad portfolio representative of the market as a whole. In the case of Fidelity (its U.S. research analysts number in the hundreds and its managers possess recognized industry knowledge and demonstrated sector stock-picking ability), you've certainly got a lot of firepower on your side. Finally, the Fidelity sector funds have a track record, whereas sector SPDRs have been available for trading less than one year. But investors should watch with interest as performance comparisons between the established active and new passive sector products become available.

Trading Notes

MERs are generally in the 2.50% range for both Fidelity and C.I. sector funds offered in Canada. NN Financial, the Dutch insurance giant, charges even more for its sector family. For the currency aware, both Fidelity and C.I. offer their funds conveniently priced in Canadian or U.S. dollars.

NEW WRINKLES: STRUCTURED INDEX FUNDS/SOCIALLY RESPONSIBLE INDEX FUNDS

In the hands of sophisticated indexers, index returns can either be enhanced or customized. Structured index funds are designed to do the former, while socially responsible index funds do the latter. In addition, structured funds make a definite appeal to investor psychology to the extent that they offer the promise of beating the index bogey. Similarly, socially responsible funds appeal to the caring/giving/feeling side of investors who want their pound of greed without an ounce of remorse.

We'll start with the supercharged index products. The next generation in index investing methodology in the U.S. is termed structured index fund management, which seeks to address some of the perceived deficiencies of a pure index approach. In this sense, structured (also termed enhanced or managed) indexing represents the next logical step in terms of what sophisticated indexers are already doing.

Marketing index thinking to individual investors has been a winning strategy for U.S. fund sponsors: somewhere between one-quarter to one-third of every new equity investment dollar is currently being committed to index products, and the U.S. index mutual fund market now boasts just under $300 billion in assets. But there are still perceived problems with index investing in the marketplace. As discussed so many times before, an index portfolio is simply incapable of outperforming its respective benchmark, and lacking a cash cushion, it is exposed to 100% market risk on the downside. Is there a better way?

Structured index funds think so. Through advanced quantitative techniques, these funds seek to outperform their target index on the upside as well as on the downside, without increasing risk and with little tracking error. Structured index funds currently exist in the U.S. market, including a couple from Scudder, which simply eliminate all companies expected to perform in the bottom 20% of the index from their index fund portfolios. Other structured or enhanced funds are virtually hedge funds. Until recently, U.S. mutual funds were debarred from short-selling. But changes to the U.S. tax code in 1997 eased restrictions on short-selling by mutual funds, giving rise to new forms of fund structure that had previously been the domain of the hedge fund industry (a hedge fund is blind pool in which high net worth investors commit substantial funds to the manager's discretion; the manager in turn runs the fund portfolio in any way in which he/she thinks money can be made. Hedge fund managers make their money from performance bonuses, which typically amount to 20-25% of all gains once they have beat the index bogey). There are two basic types of these hedge fund-style mutual funds: long-short and short-short funds. Long-short funds use both long and short positions opportunistically to maximize returns, with the fund portfolio either long or short the different index stocks or employing S&P 500 index futures, OEX or other index options and equity swaps to gain exposure to the equity market. But this strategy is not meant to be market neutral, i.e. with the long side offsetting the short side or vice versa; there are, however, market neutral funds that try to do this. Short-short or bear market funds are simply one-way (frequently wrong-way) investments that produce positive returns when the market is tumbling, often utilizing the same index financial technology as we have been discussing. As noted, the Bank of Bermuda Global Manager family has double short (geared) as well as leveraged long international market funds.

While structured funds have been available in the U.S. institutionally for years, they are a relatively newer phenomenon at the retail level. You can expect to see more. The point is that, if passive sells, passive plus should sell even better. That's why the driving force behind the trend towards structured index products is coming from the fund industry itself as it seeks new sources of revenue and profit in a mature industry environment. The bad news for investors is that these techniques command a higher fee structure than traditional index products.

For the politically correct, ethical or socially responsible funds permit investors to gain customized equity index exposure without trampling on anyone's sensibilities. In the U.S., there are two main line socially responsible funds: the Citizens Index Fund and Domini Social Equity Fund. Both funds, which are still fairly small in terms of assets, essentially cherry-pick the S&P 500 for socially responsible companies and mix them together with other stocks they've also deemed morally a-okay. The key here is "deemed." Both funds track the S&P 500, while avoiding the traditional "sin" stocks (booze and tobacco), companies that have poor records on environmental issues or participate in the defense and nuclear industries among other criteria. While no doubt every attempt has been made to appear objective in the stock selection process, what is socially responsible and what is not must ultimately be a subjective decision.

Nonetheless, these funds have reasonable MERs and pretty good numbers (example: Domini Social Equity has an average annual 3-year return of 30.5%), which must prove that the socially responsible shall inherit the earth, one day at any rate. Watch for more of this innovative kind of stuff to come to Canada in the near future.

A SOPHISTICATED INDEXER–HOW THE FED USES THE S&P 500 TO TRACK MARKET VALUATION LEVELS

Thus far we have been primarily concerned with indexes insofar as they measure market performance. But they also have predictive and valuation applications as well. The U.S. central bank (Federal Reserve Board or Fed) has developed a proprietary model for tracking the overall valuation level of the U.S. equity market. It works like this. In the Fed model, fair value for the S&P 500 is deemed to equate with projected S&P index earnings divided by the index level so as to equal the yield on the 10-year U.S. treasury bond. By this measure, the S&P 500 Index has been above fair value for most of 1998 and all of 1999.

GENTLEMEN PREFER BONDS

While the bond market is several times larger than the stock market as measured by the total value of securities traded, it is much less visible and still something of a mystery to many investors. Unlike stocks, bond pricing is almost purely mathematical and therefore predictable. But the bond market itself reflects the complex interplay of diverse forces at work in the economy, including government fiscal and monetary policy, developments in the interest rate policy of major trading partners and interest rate volatility resulting from of changes in the value of the dollar.

We won't do too much 101 here, except to try and put the essential risk of owning bonds in context. In that vein, we'll quickly remind ourselves of some fundamental characteristics of bonds, primarily in terms of the Canadian market. Bonds are the debt obligations of the federal, provincial or municipal government, a government agency or a corporation. A bond issuer's creditworthiness reflects the interest rate that can be offered to investors. Federal government, provincial, and municipal bonds are usually rated highest quality, while corporate bonds are graded under different investment categories by several bond rating services. In all cases, the issuer undertakes to pay the bondholder a specified rate of interest for a specified time, and repay the principal in full at maturity. Generally, bonds feature the following basic characteristics:

- A fixed rate of interest (coupon) usually payable semi-annually.
- A commitment to repay the principal in full when the bond matures.
- A fixed term to maturity. A bond's term to maturity is either short (1-3 years), medium (3-10 years) or long (over 10 years).

Unlike Canada Savings Bonds or GICs, government and corporate bonds are continuously bought and sold in the secondary market where they are traded; that is, they are marketable (can be sold to a second party) and not just redeemable (can be sold back only to the issuer). Because of the existence of a secondary market, bond prices fluctuate as market forces, and particularly interest rates, change. While bonds are redeemed at 100% of face value (or par) at maturity and their coupon or interest rate is fixed, their capital values change daily. Consequently, it is possible to enjoy capital gains—or experience capital losses—by investing in bonds.

In the secondary market, the main pricing mechanism for bonds is the prevailing level of interest rates, the coupon rate and term to maturity of the individual debt security, and to a lesser extent, the creditworthiness of the bond issuer, supply/demand for particular issues and general market tone. Uptrending interest rates result in higher yields and decreasing bond prices, as bond values move inversely to the direction of rates. Note also that, while bonds are usually quoted in terms of yield, they can also be quoted in terms of price.

There are two ways of calculating a bond's yield:

- Current yield is calculated as the coupon rate divided by price (just like a stock) though this is an essentially useless calculation.
- Yield to maturity is calculated as the coupon rate plus the bond's amortized discount or premium (i.e. where the bond price currently stands in relation to par); this is the yield calculation that matters to investors.

Yield to maturity must be precisely calculated by computer or a bond yield book. Also note that yield to maturity calculations assume that the bond's semi-annual interest payment is reinvested at the same rate as the coupon. Clearly, this is not always possible. With longer maturities in particular, by far the greatest return comes from reinvesting the semi-annual or annual coupon. Zero coupon bonds are the only bond investment option that can guarantee the reinvestment rate, hence the actual yield, to the investor.

The risk of investing money with greater uncertainty of return (or for longer periods of time as in the case of the bond market) usually demands some sort of risk premium as we have discussed previously. With bonds, that risk premium is reflected simply in higher yields. Generally, shorter-term maturities have lower yields while long-term (say 30 year bonds) have higher yields. This relationship can be illustrated graphically by the yield curve, which plots the differential between yields all the way along the term to maturity spectrum. If the slope of the curve reflects a linear progression of yield increases as term to maturity increases, the yield curve is said to be normal or positive. This is the relationship you would expect, as the longer the term to maturity, the higher the risk premium usually demanded by lenders or investors, hence the higher the yield.

Sometimes, however, fundamental economic factors and market forces can alter the slope of the curve. When shorter-term maturities provide a higher interest rate than longer-term maturities, the yield curve is said to be inverted. This can result from the impact of a severe recessionary environment or alternatively from central bank intervention in the money markets aimed at tightening interest rates. The situation can also arise where there is no difference between short and long-term rates as the curve moves towards or away from inversion. Here the yield curve is said to be flat, though this is a highly infrequent occurrence.

Duration–Key Risk Management Measure

The yield curve depicts the prevailing level of interest rates at each term to maturity. In turn, the central reference point for bond pricing is the level of interest rates when the bond purchase is made. Since bonds are the most purely mathematical of financial instruments, their current price must reflect the current interest rate (or yield level) of equivalent securities competing for the same investment dollar.

As we have noted, a bond has two components: the capital portion and the regular coupon income. But if you think about it slightly differently, you will almost certainly agree that a bond is essentially one thing, and that is a stream of payments owed to the bondholder: the interest rate component (a series of payments paid—usually—once every six months over the term of the investment); and the principal component (the final payment of the face value of the bond—usually multiples of $1,000). For example: a 10-year bond purchased at par with a 5% semi-annual coupon will provide the investor with 20 individual interest payments of $50 a year in two $25 instalments until it matures, at which point it would make the final $25 payment and return the $1,000 of principal originally invested. The mathematical value or price of any bond at any given time is therefore the sum of the present value of each coupon payment still outstanding plus the present value of the principal amount. Present value is the mirror image of future value (i.e. compound interest). Today's value of a future payment is the amount of that payment discounted or reduced by the interest rate currently obtainable on funds of comparable term to maturity.

Duration is the tool that measures the price sensitivity of a bond or bond portfolio to changes in the prevailing level of interest rates. Consequently, duration, which is measured in years (but not to be confused with term to maturity, see below), is the basic mathematical measure of bond portfolio volatility. If a particular bond consisted of one future payment, its term to maturity and its duration would be identical. But since most bonds consist of a series of future payments, the duration of a bond is actually the weighted average of the present value of the future stream of payments, including the final lump sum repayment of principal. Also note that the duration of a bond will always be shorter than its term to maturity except in the case of zeros or strips, when it is identical.

So duration is the key risk indicator for a bond portfolio because it measures how capital values respond to changes in rates. But there are

a couple of other things that can make duration seem especially complicated (there's more than one kind of duration to begin with). First,
duration sounds like the same as term to maturity since they are both
measured in years. But it isn't. A bond with a duration of 6.2 years will
increase about 6.2% in price if its yield drops by one percentage point
(100 basis points) or decrease 6.2% if its yield rises by 100 basis points;
in either case, its term to maturity remains the same. Furthermore,
as a bond's yield falls, its duration lengthens, indicating increased price
sensitivity; conversely as a bond's yield rises, its duration shortens,
making it less sensitive to additional changes in rates. That's common
sense, but here's another complication: as a bond's price and yield fluctuate, so does the volatility of its duration. Here's why: current yield is
the rate used to discount the bond's future payments in order to calculate present value. As yield drops, the present value of the future payments rises, with the value of the payments furthest out rising the most.
So to rebalance this situation, duration must also lengthen.

While the duration of an individual bond can be calculated, that's
not really important in and of itself; it's the duration of the bond portfolio that is of most interest to professional fixed-income investors.
Generally, bond managers compare the duration of their portfolios
to the index they are using as their benchmark. In the U.S., as we have
seen, there are several major bond indexes, the vast Lehman Brothers
Aggregate Bond Index being the most representative; in Canada,
ScotiaMcLeod's SMU Index reigns supreme.

Finally, we're coming to the point. Like stock market indexes, the
S&P 500 or whatever, the bond index represents base 100 from the
perspective of managing portfolio risk. Active bond managers may
choose to peg their portfolios at the same duration as the index itself
(this is termed a duration neutral strategy and is essentially the same
thing as closet indexing, see p. 89) or they may choose to maintain their

portfolios above the benchmark duration. You can find out this sort of information on a fund-by-fund basis by perusing individual fund company simplified prospectuses, annual reports or website updates.

So one last time, what's the point of all this fuss about duration? Duration provides the most important measure of risk available to the bond investor by calculating the sensitivity of a bond portfolio to changes in the prevailing level of interest. But it also gives investors an important cost/benefit measurement tool for active bond funds and bond index funds, both of which are after all benchmarked to the duration of the index they track. Actively managed bond funds that are duration neutral are simply much more expensive versions of bond index funds; actively managed bond funds that are maintained above the relevant bond index duration are taking on excess interest rate risk to try to enhance returns (see p. 109 for the discussion of how you should be compensated for taking on supra market risk). Gentlemen/women prefer bonds because they ensure a return of capital as well as a return on capital. The question investment consumers have to ask themselves is simply, what is the best and more cost-effective way of having appropriate bond representation in my overall portfolio mix? Bond index funds win hands down.

Investing in Bonds

Beyond the imperative of prudent asset allocation, no investor should need to be reminded about how bonds are integral to the construction and success of an overall investment portfolio, particularly in a trendless or declining equity market. Bonds pay regular coupon income regardless of what happens to their principal value as a result of negative interest rate movements, and they are less volatile than stocks. In addition, if held to maturity, bonds promise to return 100 cents on the dollar. But bonds aren't no-risk investments and it is entirely possible to lose money in the bond market. Moreover, bonds usually return less than stocks. In the U.S., for example, stocks outperformed bonds by a ratio of about 2:1 (around 18% for stocks as tracked by the S&P 500 and only 9% or so for bonds) over a recent 10-year period; in Canada, the numbers are somewhat reversed over the same time frame (approximately 11.5% for bonds versus only 9.65% for stocks), though again Canadian equity market performance has been abysmal during this period. Longer term domestic numbers indicate a modest outperformance factor for stocks over bonds as one would expect.

But that's really not the point. A portfolio of stocks combined with bonds is more risk efficient than a pure equity portfolio. The reason is that, while bonds lower portfolio returns, they also lower portfolio volatility. According to long-term U.S. data from 1972-1997, a portfolio consisting entirely of the S&P 500 returned an average of 13.1% a year, while a portfolio consisting of 25% mid-term U.S. government bonds and 75% S&P 500 stocks returned an average of 12.2% annually. That's less return all right, but the diversified portfolio also came with less risk, which is indicative of its efficiency in that it generated about the same return per unit of risk (about the same Sharpe ratio for the technically inclined).

Leaving aside for now their merits as an asset class, there are three basic ways to invest in bonds: buy cash market bonds (Canadian, U.S. treasuries, international, foreign pay bonds, etc.); buy actively managed bond funds (domestic or international); or buy bond index (U.S. or Canadian) funds. There are obvious advantages to each but there should be no mystery, dear reader, as to conclusion that has already been reached.

Active Versus Bond Index Funds

Bonds provide an even more compelling case for index investing than stocks, and for much the same reasons. The most important one again is cost. Bonds generally return less on average than stocks, so the MERs on active bond funds can eat up an even more significant part of total investment returns. The bond market is also much larger than the stock market and consequently more efficient, which means that it is even harder to add value through active fund management than is the case with equities.

Bond indexing seeks to redress this imbalance by providing diversification to the yield curve and affordability through low minimums, but at much lower expense ratios than actively managed bond funds. Herein lies the primary appeal of bond indexing. Not only are bond index fund MERs significantly lower (about 50% lower on average, which obviously contributes to better performance), but bond index funds are also generally less risky than actively managed funds because they are by definition duration neutral. As with equities, it is true that an active manager can outperform the bond index bogey, but this is possible only by taking on excess risk. It is also true that a rich fund MER eats into performance even before the market has had a chance to strut its stuff; active bond funds are also invariably load funds, which can further negatively impact total returns to investors.

It is for these reasons that many commentators and advisors in the past have recommended against buying actively managed bond funds. Instead, they suggest buying individual bonds on a laddered basis to provide diversification by term to maturity (strip bonds can do this quite effectively). The same argument applies to balanced funds for that matter. The rationale in the latter case is place 50% of your assets in an active or index equity fund and buy cash bonds with the balance because it's much cheaper than active bond management. This, however, has overlooked the bond index fund advantage. Buying individual bonds can cost big money; unless you've got deep pockets, it's difficult to achieve any sort of portfolio diversification buying a few bonds at a time; and there are hidden transaction costs along the way, even if you can save something in management fees (see below). Bond index funds, on the other hand, get you around high MERs, while ensuring the same broad diversification, investment access for a relatively small amount of money, automatic coupon reinvestment and daily liquidity that is possible with active bond funds. Consequently, we shall consider that the case has been made and look at bond index funds exclusively from here on in.

Canadian Bond Index Funds

The number of Canadian bond index funds is still small, particularly compared to the broader universe of equity index funds, but nonetheless offers some choice for the wary investment consumer. Again, the leading suppliers are TD and CIBC. Both the TD Green Line Canadian Government Bond Index Fund and the CIBC Canadian Short-Term Bond Fund have been around since 1993 and are above-average performers ranking in the top 25% of Canadian bond funds. They also have attractive MERs (80 basis points and 90 basis points respectively). CIBC also offers CIBC Canadian Bond Index Fund and its 5-year Protected Canadian Bond Index Fund equivalent. In addition, the insurance industry (Commercial Union, Zurich, NN, etc.) has contenders in the field, but like the CIBC protected funds, they charge for the privilege. The average Canadian actively managed bond fund has an MER of about 1.7%, while the insurance and protected products start at around 2% and up. The general benchmark for Canadian bond index funds is the SMU (exception: TD Green Line Canadian Government Bond Index Fund, which tracks the more specialized ScotiaMcLeod government bond index). There are also a couple of global bond funds sponsored by CIBC and NN (the big hitter in the MER department once more) which track more specialized composite international indexes. Increased competition in this sector will be good for index investors in their search for cost-effective asset class proxies.

U.S. Bond Index Funds

The key U.S. bond index fund sponsors include the Vanguard, Fidelity, Scudder, American Century, T. Rowe Price, Charles Schwab and Strong fund groups. Vanguard offers bond index products with relatively low minimums, but others have higher minimum entry levels ($10,000–$100,000). MERs currently range from 20 basis points (0.2%) on the Vanguard bond index funds to 60 basis points (0.6%) on the Schwab offerings. All have solid and long-term performance track records, the "long term" portion of which cannot be said of their Canadian equivalents.

Trading Notes

Thus far, we have not considered the case for holding individual stocks, except in passing. The bond market is different, again because of the cost structure implicit in having someone else look after your fixed-income portfolio for you. While holding bonds directly is cheaper than investing in bond funds with their big MERs, bond trading requires substantial capital (a board lot in the bond market is $25,000) to ensure any kind of portfolio diversification (by maturity) and sensible pricing. In addition, pricing in the bond market is invisible since there's no obvious commission incurred on transacting. Instead of a commission, the yield you receive from an investment dealer includes an undisclosed mark-up on the price of the bond. Another concern is the fact that the bond market is an OTC market, where price information is less readily available to individual investors than it is to institutions. Some illiquid securities are hard to price because they are seldom traded; others have enormous bid/ask spreads if you find you have to unload them in a hurry; others still are highly susceptible to market supply/ demand factors. Only the most heavily traded bonds (e.g. bellwether Government of Canadas) are immune from this. Consequently, it pays to have substantial assets and a non-life threatening investment time line before considering a foray into the cash bond market.

CHAPTER 7

Asset Allocation and

Index Investing

IF SOMETHING LIKE 70–80% of active fund managers cannot beat the leading investment benchmarks (or indexes) consistently, it may make more sense for individual investors to focus their attention on matching rather than trying to outperform the market. As the U.S. experience in 1998 clearly showed, the S&P 500 Index return was almost 29% versus average U.S. active manager returns of only around 10% (the longer-term number is, of course, higher for active U.S. managers, see Chapter 1). That's quite a spread, but in and of itself, it really isn't even the point. Nobody knows what the market is going to do in any given year, let alone whether active manager A is going to be able to beat it or not. In addition, retail investors have been paying dearly for chasing active stock selection, and not just in terms of management fees. We've already explored this and the myth of active manager outperformance in detail in the context of the U.S. and Canadian markets (also see Chapter 1).

On the other hand, index investing for both bonds and equities may provide the answer as your best means of creating efficient and cost-effective asset class exposure. But beyond good investment consumerism, the index premise in turn opens up a new way of looking at how individuals can manage their own retirement and investment portfolios by applying index thinking to their overall financial planning and asset management decision-making process. I am not a financial planner, but it makes sense to try and complete the circle by considering briefly how index principles can be put to work as part of an individual asset allocation strategy.

The whole area of asset allocation as it applies to individual investors has been so widely covered in innumerable books, articles and seminars and the like that it seems a little redundant to even attempt to make further comment, but I remain convinced that the two words are more often said than understood. As usual, the best recent discussion of this topic is again in Bogle, *Common Sense* (pp. 57 ff.); if you read nothing else, including the following, that would more than suffice.

Asset allocation itself has become something of a mini-industry in the U.S. and Canadian financial services sector since the early 1990s. On the coattails of an important article published in *Fortune* magazine in the late 1980s, which popularized contemporary academic research into portfolio performance attribution, as it is termed in the trade, all the banks, fund companies and other financial industry suppliers began offering asset allocation (AA) models or AA services designed to help investors do a better job of managing their portfolios based on fairly static risk/reward profiles and individual investor inputs. They undoubtedly served to get people thinking about their own financial circumstances, but off-the-shelf products like these, no matter how well conceived, have flaws. Perhaps the biggest problem is that they are frequently too complicated, too rigid in their risk assumptions, stick too closely to precise bond and stock allocations and, most of all, underestimate the age until which individual investors should stay invested in equities. Consider this sort of prototypical AA profile based on age and imputed risk tolerance levels which you've probably seen a thousand times before in fund company brochures or magazine articles:

Asset Allocation—The New Way to Determine How You Should Invest Your Portfolio, Blah, Blah, Blah

Successful asset allocation depends on your age, investment time horizon and risk tolerance. Compare your situation to these typical asset allocation profiles:

Age 35: 60% stock funds, 30% bond funds and 10% cash or GICs.

Age 45: 50% stock funds, 35% bond funds and 15% cash or GICs.

Age 55: 40% stock funds, 40% bond funds and 20% cash or GICs.

This sort of thing is fine as far as it goes, but it's really nothing more than a crude navigational aid. There are several other so-called "rules of thumb" about asset class exposure. Take the 100-year rule, which produces approximately the same sort of result as above. This old chestnut goes like this: to find out what proportion of your portfolio you should have invested in stocks at any point in your life, subtract your age from 100; the remaining number reflects the approximate level of equity exposure appropriate for your age (and imputed risk tolerance) level. By this measure, at age 40, you should be 60% invested in stocks and 40% in bonds. At 60, 40% stocks and 60% bonds, etc. For some, this could work, but for others it may make no sense at all. An allocation of 40% fixed income for a 40 year old looks exceptionally conservative to me. But that's the problem with trying to use an asset allocation formula that's based on the principle that one size fits all.

On this latter point, investors naturally become more conservative as they approach retirement, but there is no magical moment when you should dump equities and raise cash. Even with the low inflation rates we have been enjoying in North America in recent years, inflation still poses a threat and the primary danger for many retirees is not necessarily what you would expect. Consider the demographic facts. In 1965, the average retirement age was 65; based on Canadian mortality statistics from that period, the average retiree lived fewer than eight years in retirement. Today, the average retirement age is about 62, while retirees are living approximately 22 years and even longer into retirement. The good news is that people are living much longer. The bad news is that you could risk outliving your investment capital in retirement as a result, and this is perhaps the most serious challenge in all retirement planning today. The destruction of purchasing power over time should be one of any retiree's biggest concerns, and the potential for outliving retirement capital should be a prime consideration in establishing your personal financial plan. Even with just a 3% annual inflation rate (which is well below the Canadian average since 1950), the value of a portfolio is reduced in real terms by 35% over a 10-year period. Since even comparatively low rates of inflation can be guaranteed to erode purchasing power, you will need to ensure that your income is actually growing in retirement to maintain your current standard of living, i.e. just to stay on an even keel. It is for this reason (plus low interest rates) that annuities have made so little sense in recent years and self-directed RIFs, which permit individualized asset allocation including the freedom to maintain the degree of equity exposure that works for each investor, have become the exit strategy of choice for Canadian RSP investors.

Another rule of thumb approach for establishing personal asset mix parameters is playing the percentages game. Since it's a given that you won't know precisely how much money you will actually need to retire in any sort of comfort—even in year one—you should simply assume that you will require about 70% of your pre-retirement income. This assumption is intended to make life easy, though I have noticed at least one leading Canadian actuary questioning its validity. Seventy percent of $100,000, for example, is $70,000. In the most naïve and simple terms, funding an annual pension of $70,000 would require retirement capital of $700,000 at an absolute minimum based on a 10% annual investment return. Obviously, that doesn't take into account any sort of inflation or margin of error factor. So the question that is really left unanswered by this approach is, how much can you save— and how much can you earn on your savings—to generate the retirement income you will need?

Then there's the good old fashioned household cash flow forecasting approach which appeals to the latent accountant in all of us. This is what the bank and other comparable planning models attempt to do by getting you to try to forecast your future income, expenditures, liabilities, inheritances, taxes and so on. How much money will you need to live? How much do you want to leave for your children or heirs? Are you going to stay in the house or downsize and therefore free up capital? Do you have any major purchases that you want to make to improve/change your lifestyle in retirement? Are you going to become a world traveler or just sit it out at the cottage, etc. etc.? Then when you've got all this figured out once and for all, you are asked to try to determine what level of return on capital you will need to achieve your financial/lifestyle goals and assess the level of risk you are willing to take on to achieve them. Risk, as always, is measured in terms of your exposure to the stock market.

Many of the leading mutual fund companies, financial institutions and financial planners provide their asset allocation models and asset class return calculators gratis either in print format or via the Internet to help you do this. After calculating your future living expenses and projected life expectancy, you must determine an annual rate of return for your investments using various rate calculations/assumptions. To do so, you will need to know the actual current or projected opening balance of your retirement portfolio, the closing balance (i.e. what will be left at the time of your hypothetical death), how much money you will withdraw every year and the number of periods (i.e. how many years, months, etc.) you intend to use your systematic withdrawal plan or equivalent. Remember that this calculation does not factor in the impact of inflation (some, however, like the useful Fidelity website can), but it will give you a rough-and-ready fix on your probable retirement income. This process also doesn't take into account any periodic port-folio rebalancing, but that's just another complication. Once you have completed your initial asset allocation strategy (so much to stocks, so much to bonds, etc.), it may not be necessary to rebalance your assets very often, but you should periodically review your portfolio, say at least once a year or as market conditions warrant. The net result of this exercise should be to suggest the portfolio that is specifically designed to reflect the kind of investor you really are or want to become over time; or at least, that's the theory.

Balanced funds, which are really crude asset allocation products, have been around for years, but fund giant AGF launched one of the first Canadian asset allocation services in the early 1990s based on dynamic asset allocation principles. The AGF product employs a computer-driven model that determines the comparative attractiveness of the three principal asset classes based on fair value calculations—essentially comparing the current and historical long-term bond yield versus the discounted equity index dividend yield—and then automatically switches from least to most attractive asset class as frequently as re-quired. The problem with asset allocation services of this kind is that they are still based on three active funds for stocks, bonds and money market, and are consequently an expensive way to benefit from asset allocation. All of the major Canadian FIs (financial institutions) have excellent personal asset allocation planning models available in booklet or web form as well as extensive support literature, but they too are ultimately designed to try to get you to place your money in their funds. In itself, this is not a bad thing, because the big banks and trust companies have been responsible for bringing index investing to Canadian investors, but it is reality. Mackenzie's STAR program is more elaborate still, proposing to create several different optimized portfolios based on quantitatively driven strategic asset allocation principles; it has enjoyed considerable marketing success. One of the most interesting approaches it that offered by the financial website imoney (www.imoney.com), which simply wants to know what you've got in the way of assets and then suggests what you can do with them to help you achieve your goals.

The problem with many of these approaches is that they force you to make assumptions based on uncertainties viewed against an even still more unpredictable future (compare Churchill on the Soviet Union: a riddle wrapped in a mystery inside an enigma, etc.) It is readily acknowledged that the ultimate composition of your retirement portfolio and the asset allocation decisions you make depend on many obvious factors, including your investment time horizon, your financial needs and personal lifestyle requirements. But that is the key to asset allocation in the first place. It is an intensely personal and consequently imprecise kind of assessment unless you are possessed of an actuary living in your attic for daily consultations.

Any "black box" approach entails asking a lot of questions, quantifying your answers and then creating a portfolio based on the most "efficient frontier" for Every Investor (an efficient frontier consists of the best mix of stocks, bonds and cash given an investor's risk tolerance level, see p. 109). Most of these AA programs, however, suffer from two flaws: they require you to input your own return expectations with little or no guidance as to how to make a reasonable estimate about them in the first place; and they provide no means of connecting your investment strategy (which is the key determinant of your return expectations) with your overall financial plan. A black box, moreover, cannot understand your personal needs or deal with many of the subjective judgments that are part of understanding your unique situation. Nonetheless, while the asset allocation process is perforce a best efforts type of exercise, the principles of index investing can help you get at least in the direction of where you want to be.

FROM THEORY TO PRACTICE

You've seen the fund company brochures: Asset allocation seeks to ensure that your funds are invested in the right financial assets in the right proportion at the right time. Asset allocation puts the power of modern computer technology and the statistical probability of investment success firmly on your side. Asset allocation provides the opportunity for superior investment performance but with less volatility than is typically experienced from each of the individual asset classes on their own—a process that can be complex, time-consuming and error-prone even for investment professionals. A trip to the moon on gossamer wings, anyone?

That is a tall order. But as we have seen, it has been overwhelmingly demonstrated by academic research that asset allocation is the primary factor behind investment success, accountable for as much as 90% of the differential among comparative portfolio returns. The problem, of course, lies not with the theory, it is in the execution.

In a nutshell, when you are constructing your retirement or investment portfolio, you must bear two overriding considerations in mind: your portfolio return must be sufficient to enable you to reach your financial objectives, otherwise you're simply going to be short of the ready (this is charmingly termed "insufficiency risk" in the pension industry); and as we all know, the government isn't going to be taking care of you. This reality will of necessity involve you with all the different asset classes unless you're starting off rich (stocks outperform bonds, bonds outperform cash, etc.) But you should also factor into your asset allocation decision-making the degree of risk you can sleep with (this is termed the SWAN or sleep well at night principle) and that is the second constraint. Otherwise, you're bound to become a slave to irrational anxiety and in the throes of emotional overdrive may be tempted to change strategy recklessly or without giving full consideration to the implications of any change in plan. As Bogle says, staying the course is the most important determinant of the success of any personal asset allocation strategy ("Stay the course. It is the most important single piece of investment wisdom I can give you").

Asset allocation also mandates that you should have your portfolio invested in each asset class in proportion to your basic risk tolerance level—all the time. That is to say, no market timing is allowed. A typical asset mix could be 50% stock index funds, 40% bond index funds and 10% money market funds or GICs; these numbers themselves don't matter, what matters is the allocation that makes sense for you. Since you're not trying to time the market, you're invested all the time and continue to commit funds on a periodic basis through dollar-cost averaging or any other sort of regular investment savings program essentially in proportion to your original asset mix strategy. You can modify your allocations as returns from one asset class begin to outgrow your target mix level (i.e. requiring you to rebalance your portfolio) or as your personal circumstances change, but you should avoid doing so simply because changing market conditions may seem to warrant doing so (i.e. you are panicking because of short-term volatility).

In order to arrive at any sort of preliminary asset allocation decisions, of course, there are some necessary personal inputs. Let's look at them informally and then formally, in human terms and then in number crunching terms. First, the informal personal questions you need to ask yourself:

1. How much money do you need to get what you want out of life, especially as you near retirement, in addition to your regular income (pension income?) if you are still working? Nothing outlandish, but you probably have a mortgage to pay off, several more cars to buy, your children's education and marriages to fund, a leisure time cottage or other property to acquire/divest yourself of, vacations or exotic travel to enjoy, and, oh yes, the little matter of a (secondary or entire) retirement income.

2. How much do you think you'll need overall and how much specifically for each item you have identified? Nothing too precise, ball park will do.

3. How much can you put away/save/invest over the entire period and over the various individual time periods leading up to your retirement (i.e. can you "calendarize" your projected savings and expenditures over the next few years?) Nothing too detailed, just concentrate on the big picture and big ticket items such as the mortgage, cottage and so on.

4. How much is the difference between what you think you'll have and what you think you'll need? This is the painful one.

5. How much will you have to make on your investments to earn the money you think you'll need? This is your reality check.

Asset allocation decision-making is really no more complicated than this. In financial plannerese, these steps equate with the following:

1. What are the investor's overall investment objectives, investment time horizon, personal constraints and risk tolerance level?
2. What are rational expectations for comparative asset class returns over the investor's time horizon based on historical and anticipated asset class performance?
3. What is the outlook for the macro-economic environment, inflation and other market-related forces that will impact comparative asset class returns during this time period?
4. What are the investor's income and capital growth expectations, tax status, liquidity constraints, etc.?
5. What is the optimal mix of securities to be utilized in the investor's personal asset allocation strategy on a risk-adjusted basis, and what are the indicated proportionate weightings to which the portfolio should be periodically rebalanced?

Understanding Asset Classes for Children

Let's recap all of this in very simple terms (if this sounds childish, je m'excuse, but the subject of asset mix is too frequently treated as mumbo-jumbo). Asset allocation means investing in the right mix of assets—stocks for capital growth, fixed income for a balance of secure income and growth and cash for security—in the right proportion corresponding to your long-term needs. Consider the common sense/common language case for creating exposure to all asset classes in some proportion in your asset allocation process first. With stocks, you know you will experience short-term pain for long-term gain because stocks exhibit the highest degree of short-term volatility with the highest long-term performance track record (see p. 176). With bonds, you have security of principal in the long term, but price volatility in the short term as interest rates change, though usually considerably less so than with stocks. With cash, you have total security of principal but generally a relatively low yield or rate of return. The problem is, you can never tell which asset class will outperform at any given point because you can't predict what the market will do (no one can time the market). What you can do is control your exposure to the market. And that's what asset allocation is really all about. While there are also secondary asset classes (precious metals, art and collectibles, wine futures, real estate, etc.), the major asset classes employed by Canadian investment professionals in pension fund management and so on number just three:

- Cash for security—high-quality, short-term federal or provincial government T-Bills, Bankers' Acceptances, Commercial Paper and other government and corporate money market instruments.
- Fixed income for a balance of secure income and capital growth— domestic and international government bonds, including federal, provincial and municipal issues, investment grade corporate bonds, high yield issues, residential mortgages, mortgage-backed securities and preferred shares.
- Stocks for growth—(a) Active: common shares of major Canadian and international companies listed on recognized stock exchanges. (b) Index: the securities or futures contracts that comprise the leading Canadian and U.S. stock market indexes. (c) Balanced: a combination of stocks, bonds and money market securities, usually with up to 20% foreign content. (d) International: either actively or index managed, usually a portfolio of leading global big-cap companies.

Within each major asset class, there are, of course, subclasses. For instance, with stocks, there are large-cap, mid-cap and small-cap companies as we have seen. There are also growth stocks and value stocks. There are short-, mid- and long-term bonds, etc., etc. Indexes—investable ones at that, particularly in the U.S.—exist for just about all of these subclasses, which should provide the implementation vehicles you require to implement your own asset allocation strategy (see pp. 180 ff. in the next chapter).

If you were omnipotent and could pick the best-performing asset class or subclass at any given time, you would clearly enjoy the greatest return, but you would also most certainly be incurring the highest level of risk as well. So to control risk but still reach your financial goals, you can't put all your eggs in one basket and must instead allocate your funds among the different asset classes. The performance of each asset class should offset weakness in any of the others and serve to complement their strengths. It should also help reduce overall portfolio risk.

The relationship between cash and bonds is fairly straightforward. Generally, both are the children of the current interest rate environment. If short-term rates increase, usually but not always longer-term rates will increase as well and vice versa if rates fall. The interrelationship between stocks and bonds is much more complicated. There are many explanations as to why stocks move in the same direction as bonds (e.g. declining interest rates), move in the opposite direction to bonds (e.g. resurgent inflation) or simply do not correlate at all. The latter is almost certainly the correct answer: there is simply no statistically significant correlation in terms of the change in bond prices and that of the equity markets on either a short- or long-term basis.

Be that as it may, since the ultimate goal of asset allocation is not a matter of beating the market(s) but rather producing a return on capital that will address your long-term financial needs with the least amount of risk, effective asset allocation involves investors in a portfolio construction process that is also affected by a number of important external factors of which individuals should at least be aware and in a general sort of way pay attention to.

MACRO-ECONOMIC FACTORS THAT IMPACT COMPARATIVE ASSET CLASS PERFORMANCE

How economists measure the economy has a profound impact on the way the various asset classes perform and interrelate. While no one except professional money managers should be worrying about these factors on a day-by-day basis, they can influence your asset allocation decision-making in the broadest sense:

- GDP (gross domestic product) or more specifically the rate of economic growth. The stock and bond markets like moderate, sustainable economic growth. Excessive growth puts upward pressure on interest rates with negative consequences for all major asset classes except cash (the pattern is usually: bonds down as interest rates rise/stocks initially down but then frequently up on the basis that they are the only store of value in an inflationary environment/short-term yields up, which is good for T-bill investors). Weak growth results in essentially the opposite scenario.
- CPI or inflation. Since consumer spending represents over 60% of total GDP, this measure of inflation is keenly watched and is the number one enemy of the bond market. Central banks increase short-term (so-called "administered") rates

to put the brakes on inflation should it become a factor, giving rise to the asset class knee-jerk response sketched above.

- Productivity gains. This is an increasingly widely watched economic indicator (based on what the average worker produces per hour) of how fast the economy can grow without inflationary pressures emerging. Recently, productivity in the U.S. has been rising at a 2.5% annual rate, which means that wages can go up a corresponding amount with no inflationary implications. The Internet age's ultimate legacy to the old boom and bust world economy may be the possibility for relatively strong growth and little inflation as we move towards a service-oriented economy. The result could be a prolonged, Eisenhower era-style bull market for both stocks and bonds.

- Fed funds rate/Bank of Canada rate. The brakes or the throttle that the central bankers can place on the locomotive of national economic growth. Short-term rates impact the money supply, the amount of credit available to companies and individuals, T-bill yields, the level of the dollar and so on, but while they reflect one measure of the current level of inflation (i.e. the cost of money), they are not directly indicative of investors' concerns about inflation (the bond market does this job). Upward pressure on short-term rates is negative for both stock and bond markets, although of course this is good for cash investors.

- Bond market yields. Since they are pure market instruments, longer-term government and corporate bonds generally reflect investors' inflationary expectations. Any increase in long-term bond yields (and corresponding weakness in bond prices) is a direct reflection of investors' inflation concerns, but also (since higher interest rates slow economic growth) represent the potential cure for inflation even if it takes a while to work its way through the system. The current level of bond market yields is also crucial to the valuation of the equity market. The old rule of thumb is that anything north of 7% on the U.S. long bond (the bellwether 30-year Treasury) should put a cap on stock prices since the risk-adjusted bond yield is preferable to the return potential from stocks. As the market of last resort, bonds take on a (very profitable) life of their own in a crisis as the fallout from the Asian contagion and the collapse of Long Term Capital in the fall of 1998 attest.

- The dollar. A nation's currency is the barometer of domestic interest rates and national trade surpluses/deficits. When either the Canadian or U.S. dollar goes up in value against other major currencies, domestic goods become more expensive on world markets, slowing the domestic economy and lessening the odds of higher interest rates. There are broad implications here for the stock market, usually negative, whereas bonds should fare better on the expectation of no rate hikes.

- Commodity prices. As Canadians as well aware, higher prices for base metals (copper, nickel and aluminum), oil and forest products imply a strengthening global economy and consequently rising interest rates as increased prices in the cyclical sector reflect the fact that world industry is running on all cylinders. Commodity price pressure has historically been a key mover of Canadian equity prices.

- Money supply. During the Paul Volcker years of high inflation and high interest rates in the early 1980s, this was the premier leading indicator of inflation, hence for the bond and stock markets as a whole. While central banks still set monetary growth targets, they are now of less general importance than the direction of short-term interest rates on the market.

- Stock market valuations. If the market looks overheated, then central bankers may feel that interest rates have to rise to subdue "irrational exuberance." On the other hand, rising stock values make people think they have dollars in their pockets, and they are accordingly inclined to spend more. This is termed the wealth effect. The central bankers, particularly in the U.S., have developed a nifty measure of stock market over- and undervaluation that is monitored on a regular basis (see Chapter 6, *The Sophisticated Indexer*).

IS YOUR WAY THE BETTER WAY?

Perhaps Frank Sinatra was the original asset allocator—after all, he did it his way. Any financial planning practitioner will tell you what you already know but may not wish to hear, and that is that the only way to take control of your financial future is to try to define your own personal financial goals and then set out to achieve them. The first thing to do in this process is to disabuse yourself of the idea of scoring big time with hot stocks or setting out to beat the market bogey or whatever. The whole competitive idea of "winning" should be alien to individual investors because the odds are simply not in your favour. Consequently, trying to beat the TSE 300 or the S&P 500 or whatever should not be your priority; investing, after all, isn't a football game. Investors who think in these terms are simply the slaves of a gambling mentality and are throwing away the keys away to rational investment premises, expectations and experience.

But before you can do serious and intelligent investing, you have to do some serious and intelligent financial planning on your own. The most important but difficult part of this process is defining your personal risk tolerance level, surely the most subjective of all exercises. There is no set formula to follow here. Managing our natural greed for gain along with our innate fear of the unknown (volatility of returns in an investment context) or of failure (losing money) is essentially a psychological exercise that takes one deep into one's own subconscious self. That's why many commentators generally try to avoid this aspect of the asset allocation process, since it's much easier to say "asset allocation is a good thing" rather than tell people, particularly in print, how they can make it work in their own investment lives.

On the greed side, don't make unrealistic assumptions about what is doable and what isn't. Let's revert to our previous example of the $70,000 pension and consider someone who thinks that amount of retirement income is attainable. If you are 40 today and want to work to age 65, you've got 25 years to save your total retirement capital of $700,000. If your RSP is currently worth around $200,000, that still means you've got to amass $500,000 in round numbers to get you where you want to be. Leaving aside your existing retirement stake and forgetting about other pension income or the impact of inflation for the moment, you are going to have to save a minimum of about $5,000 per year and regularly earn 10% on your investment compounded over 25 years to make up that total with a little cushion on the side (see below for your historical chances of doing that by asset class).

In this case, your investment success and the success of your personal asset allocation strategy can best be measured by achieving your target growth rate of 10% a year. The index performance benchmark for your portfolio is consequently 10%—your personal best—not what the market is doing. Every year you achieve your 10% return threshold, your asset allocation strategy has been successful. Any year you make less than 10%, it isn't. In a strong market environment, such as in the U.S. recently, it has been entirely possible to achieve that kind of return and a lot more; and over time, 10% also equates pretty well with the historical long-term average market return. But over discrete periods of time, that has not always been the case and most certainly will not always be the case.

All the index benchmarks we have talked about so far—the S&P 500 or the TSE 300 for example—are ultimately relevant to individual investors as enabling vehicles, but they are not directly relevant to your personal goals. In effect, the various equity and bond indexes are The Market, the pond you must fish in to achieve your 10% return. Your 10% benchmark determines the level of investment risk you must take on and consequently what proportions of your portfolio you must allocate to stocks, bonds and cash as you initiate and maintain your personal asset allocation strategy on an ongoing basis. But that's what you should be focused on, not 28.7% or 13.5% or whatever.

History is there to guide you, but not much else (see below).

Finally, don't be afraid to talk to a broker or financial planner about what you are doing or want to do. Hackneyed advice as it may seem, even if you end up coming away with a black box solution, just being able to verbalize your asset allocation decision-making process could be enough. In contrast, one strikingly negative side-effect of the rise of the "do-it-yourself" investor is that you have no one to talk to. Professional money is managed, if not by committee, then through a collegial process that involves all sorts of inputs from peers, clients, external experts, third-party research and so on. It's lonely out there when you're on your own.

In sum, your personal asset allocation strategy can be effected through a simple 5-step process (and a composite of the two foregoing):

1. Review your long-term financial needs; determine your risk/return parameters; create your own individual investment plan.
2. Construct your index portfolio based on your return requirements and individual risk/return profile.
3. Select core index products for at least two of the three principal asset classes and specialized sector, sub-index or related products if appropriate.
4. Keep your eyes out for what's happening in the economy as a whole and the market in particular, but don't become a slave to it.
5. Conduct regular analysis of your portfolio performance and rebalance your portfolio if it gets out of kilter on a risk/reward basis.

Average Annual U.S. and Canadian
Primary Asset Class Returns 1973-98

The problem with comparative asset class returns—and consequently precise asset allocation—is history. What's past is not necessarily prologue. Consider these longer-term (25-year) comparative performance numbers for the major U.S. and Canadian asset classes. The shorter-term, fixed-income returns are particularly surprising, but don't forget that North American interest rates were at nearly all-time highs during this period and certainly way out of sync with historical numbers. Projecting out into the future, do you believe there is a high degree of probability that these 25-year returns are likely to be replicated and consequently can help you make an informed asset allocation decision? Or has there been a paradigm shift—i.e. is the normal return from the S&P 500 now around 30% per annum and from the long U.S. bond 6% as it has been in recent years?—not what the historical stock/bond returns and the portfolio allocations based on those returns would indicate at all? Alternatively, will the hot markets of the past few years subside and begin to re-flect the previous trend line (this is termed reversion to the mean)? Since the point of asset allocation is building an "efficient" portfolio which matches your risk tol-erance level with the most appropriate return vehicles, you are always stuck with this conundrum:

U.S. Short-term Bonds:	9.70%
U.S. Long-term Bonds:	9.60%
S&P 500 Index:	13.5%
U.S. Mid-Cap Stocks:	13.2%
U.S. Small-Cap Stocks:	13.0%
EAFE (international):	12.2%
Canadian 3-month T-bills:	9.26%
TSE 300 Composite Index:	10.91%
SMU Universe Bond Index:	10.78%

CHAPTER 8

Advanced

Index Investing

IT'S ALL THERE

Wilshire 5000 Index
Dow Jones Industrial Average
S&P 100 Index
S&P 500 Index
S&P 500/BARRA Value Index
S&P 500/BARRA Growth Index
S&P MidCap 400 Index
S&P SmallCap 600 Index
S&P Super Composite 1500 Index
Russell 1000 Index
Russell 2000 Index
Russell 3000 Index
Nasdaq Composite Index

> Nasdaq 100 Index
> TSE 300 Composite Index
> Toronto 35 Index
> S&P/TSE 60 Index
> Lehman Brothers Aggregate Bond Index
> SCM Universe Bond Index

Somebody once reportedly asked Picasso to write his autobiography. He complied by sending back a sheet of paper with all the letters of the alphabet inscribed on it. Picasso's comment: it's all there. Similarly, investors seeking to implement their own personal asset allocation strategies through index investing principles need look no farther than the list above. It's all (or just about all) there.

While we have already covered many aspects of advanced index investing, it is still possible to look at our subject in a slightly different light. I'm actually proposing to do so in three different lights or more appropriately on three different levels. In fact, these means of approach roughly correspond to the way professional pension or other institutional managers think about the way they manage assets on behalf of their fund beneficiaries. Each of these approaches is essentially based on time (i.e. investment time horizon); some fit more on the trading rather than the pure investing end of the asset management spectrum and admittedly contain an element of market timing:

1. Strategic index investing: buying and holding index funds or index participation units as part of a long-term asset allocation strategy. See *The Buy and Hold Index Investor* on p. 181.
2. Tactical index investing: buying and holding index funds or index participation units but also using index derivatives for market participation and employing index participation units and index

derivatives to hedge market risk (for taxable accounts only, i.e. this is not possible or advisable for RSP holders). See *The Hedged Index Investor* on p. 190.

3. Dynamic index investing: holding cash as well as index participation units and using index derivatives to trade domestic, U.S. and global markets dynamically and/or to hedge index portfolios. See *The Index Trader* on p. 199.

Obviously, the primary purpose of this book is to try to illustrate the wisdom of using indexes as proxies for the major asset classes, while at the same time encouraging investors to forget about trying to beat the market and utilizing index products instead to implement their long-term asset allocation strategies. But as we have seen, indexing doesn't have to be a one-dimensional approach to investing in that there are numerous indexes to benchmark to; and that choice(s) should be a result of your own asset allocation decision-making. For instance, investing in the S&P 500 or Toronto 35 as your proxy for the large-cap component of the equity marketplace almost certainly makes sense for any diversified portfolio, but these are not the only indexes available. Investors, particularly in the U.S., have the luxury of choice that enables them to create personalized index portfolios. As a result, each individual's index strategy can differ markedly, but the ideal index/mix of indexes will ultimately be based on your own asset allocation strategy; there is no other.

It's an evident enough point, and we've made it already with bonds (see pp. 144 ff.), but most index products permit investment strategies that are identical to those associated with holding all the common shares that constitute a given index in the same proportions or weightings. The only constraint is that it is much cheaper to buy an index fund or equivalent rather than a minimum of 100 shares (a board lot) each of 500 or 300 or even just 35 individual stocks. In addition, the amount of money required to buy cash market participation in one index could be more readily spread around among several different indexes using index funds, SPDRs, sector SPDRs, etc.

Once you've made the decision to employ indexes as your proxies for the major asset classes, you can create your own index portfolio of Canadian equity, Canadian bonds, U.S. equity, U.S. fixed income, international equity, etc., etc. There are also several different ways to look at constructing a portfolio consisting entirely of index funds, partially of index funds or one based on a mix of passive and active products. Finally, your investment time horizon along with your appetite for risk in the form of leverage (not volatility of returns this time) dictate the appropriateness of some of the more sophisticated index product options you have at your disposal (the latter two sections of this chapter, *The Hedged Index Investor* and *The Index Trader*, will be of interest only to this type of investor).

STRATEGIC INDEX INVESTING:
THE BUY AND HOLD INVESTOR

Sensible investors are increasingly using index products as their proxies for exposure to the various asset classes over their investment time horizon. But beyond purchasing a particular Canadian or U.S. index mutual fund or index participation units as "buy and hold," long-term investment vehicles, there are other complementary strategies that work around the corners of index principles with the potential of achieving value-added results. One of the most popular is constructing a portfolio with an index core along with other index and/or active options (this is appropriately termed "core and explore").

There are several variations on the core and explore theme, which include combining index products with: a) other index funds of different styles; b) actively managed funds; or even c) individual stocks or other equity products such as LEAPS or individual stock options. If you think of a portfolio as being something like a trimaran, the central hull portion is the passive index core while the "outriggers" are the explore portion of the portfolio. A simple example would be core SPDRs plus a U.S. small-cap index fund or even some active stock selection (say tech stocks, e.g. Microsoft, Intel, etc.) as explore.

By creating a core portfolio using index funds or products, investors retain the primary benefits of indexing (broad market representation, portfolio diversification, low-cost/low-turnover equity exposure, etc.). But they also get more, since the explore part of the equation can then be employed for further diversification or indeed to add value by providing the possibility of enhancing overall returns by beating the market in that portion of the investor's holdings. There is no contradiction here. On the point about diversification, an index fund is indeed diversified, but the sophisticated investor will think carefully about the limitations of the form of diversification each index provides (see various, but discussion on pp. 126 ff. in particular). In addition, it would be pointless not to consider what style options the various indexes represent. Similarly on the point about "beating the market," the philosophy of index investing is indeed opposed to this kind of mentality, but human nature necessarily isn't. Core and explore, at least in its passive/active incarnation, permits investors to make a very calculated bet on market sectors or individual names which may add incremental returns to their portfolios over and above the index return. But the explore portion is probably only going to account for about 10–20% of total holdings for most investors, thus limiting the overall portfolio's risk to the pitfalls of active security or sector selection.

Consequently, the pure index advantage will still accrue to the majority of the investor's portfolio. Notwithstanding our previous discussion about the dangers of Riverboat Jim-style investment thinking, the selective use of "value-added" index strategies (such as core and explore or structured index products) is appropriate at least for some investors.

The best guide to help you go about building your core portfolio or thinking about what to include in the explore portion is called style analysis, and its principles can be readily applied to both Canadian or U.S. portfolios. Again sticking with U.S. examples for the moment, a very convenient place to start is with Morningstar's website (see p. 6); hot link to the "style-rating boxes," which break the U.S. equity market down into various style categories (large, medium and small market cap; value, growth and broadly diversified, etc.). The style box approach weighs both the market cap of an individual fund's holdings as well as the manager's style, and performance is ranked over several different historical time periods.

Le style, c'est l'index lui'même

For index investors, the major indexes themselves serve as the essential building blocks for your foray into style analysis and a variety of index investment product has been built around each. The most important thing is to focus on the salient characteristics of each index. There are very significant differences. Remember that in the U.S. market, the S&P 500 consists of 500 large-cap stocks, representing approximately 70% of the total value of the U.S. stock market. The Russell 2000 Index consists of the 2,000 smallest of the 3,000 largest U.S. companies. The broadest index of all is the Wilshire 5000, which consists basically of all traded U.S. stocks, and thus represents virtually the entire U.S. stock market.

So an S&P 500 index fund is most suitable for investors looking for diversified large-cap exposure, not for the performance of smaller companies or for that matter of the market as a whole. But you can get even more specific than that (again more Vanguard examples). Vanguard Index Growth is a large-cap growth fund, but includes only that portion of the S&P 500 that is growth (i.e. not value) oriented. Similarly, Vanguard and the other U.S. suppliers have funds that track either the Russell 2000 or S&P SmallCap 600 for small-cap investors and S&P MidCap 400 product for mid-cap players. Value and growth styles are also available for the entire S&P and Russell index complexes.

This tremendous index fund variety has many advantages. For instance, there is always a great debate between large-cap and small-cap advocates. We have seen (p. 176) that the long-term returns from the two style polarities are actually pretty close. On the other hand, there will be times when small-caps outperform the large-caps, mid-caps outperform small-caps and large-caps outperform both. By judiciously choosing among the various style options, investors can hedge their bets accordingly. In the same vein, there will be times when the broader market beats the big caps, so something like the Vanguard Total Stock Market Fund which is the proxy for the Wilshire 5000 will outperform an S&P 500 index fund under those circumstances. (Note that in the competitive U.S. market, Wilshire Associates, the creator of the actual index, recently launched its own Wilshire 5000 Index Fund, while Fidelity and T. Rowe Price both offer their own versions of a U.S. total market index fund. The TSE 300 is Canada's closest equivalent to a total market index, and indexing in Canada has been based on it because there was nothing else, but I doubt if the indexing trend in this country will favour a large unwieldy index like this much longer.)

If all of this is obvious, then it's meant to be. The point is that investors must understand what indexes have been designed to do and then shop around for the indexes that most appropriately meet their needs. Large portfolios in particular can benefit from this kind of index diversification. On the other hand, sometimes just one will do. For an investor who simply wants broad exposure to the overall U.S. equity market, the Total Stock Market Fund (Bogle says that the Wilshire 5000 is increasingly becoming the equity index benchmark in the U.S.) may be all that is required. But most investors should also have some exposure to small-cap and mid-cap stocks, as well as to their more focused, big-cap brethren (the big bad S&P 500 again— you gotta love it, but you gotta understand it). There is, after all, an inevitability about the S&P 500 for index investors' portfolios.

While prudent asset allocation dictates that no investor should ever entirely abandon any asset class or investment style (large-cap, small-cap, value or growth, etc.), the trick is to determine how you want to allocate your assets accordingly. That's not an easy choice to make and there can be long periods when investors rue the day they did diversify their holdings. While the longer-term numbers seem to indicate a high degree of parallelism between small-, mid- and large-cap stock performance, you can always find periods when this breaks down. Hence prudent investors must make their own minds up about how much emphasis to place on the predictive nature of history when making their allocations or alternatively whether it makes more sense to go with the market flow and be prepared to change (I didn't say market time) index fund allocations more frequently.

Another sophistication involves making true apples to apples comparisons. As we have seen in the discussion of what asset allocation should really mean to the individual investor (i.e. it's about earning your 10% per year—in other words, investment performance is a matter of delivering a total portfolio return), the investor's focus should be on his/her overall portfolio, not its constituent parts. Complaining that your small-cap index fund has underperformed your S&P 500 fund is ridiculous; the only real question is how much did it lag the Russell 2000 Index, its appropriate benchmark. Index funds can "lag" the market (i.e. the current index market leader), but they can still perform well in terms of their benchmark and that's why you want to invest in them in the first place.

That's also why it is essentially unfair to compare the performance of an index such as the S&P 500 against that of broadly diversified active fund managers. By necessity, many active managers are obliged to invest in small-cap as well as large-cap stocks. In a market where large-cap stocks are outperforming and holders of small-cap equities are getting punished, there's no question that funds that are indexed to the winners are going to look a lot better than actively managed funds that invest in the broader market, including currently underperforming small-cap stocks.

Now that active equity funds have re-entered the discussion, many U.S. commentators believe that actively managed funds can add the most value in the small-cap and international asset class sectors. Since these areas of the market are less efficient and under-followed from a research perspective compared to large-cap stocks, living, breathing small-cap and global portfolio managers have a better chance of adding value and outperforming their appropriate benchmarks than their S&P 500-fixated brethren. The big-cap sector, on the other hand, is more efficient and sufficiently scrutinized that most active managers have a difficult time beating the broader indexes, a point we have made time and again. The comparative numbers seem to bear this out. Over the past 10 years, only something like 56 (or just over 10%) out of a universe of 537 actively managed U.S. equity funds outperformed the S&P 500, while active small-cap funds did comparatively much better against their bogey (with 51 out of 72 actively managed small-cap funds actually outperforming the Russell 2000).

There has recently been new fund development in the U.S. that indicates that the mainline suppliers are getting the message about investors' growing interest in having access to index diversity in a variety of different packages. The brand new Fidelity Four-in-One Index is a "fund of funds" product (i.e. a fund which invests exclusively in other funds), comprising four existing index funds. Its mandate is to allocate 55% of its assets to the Spartan Market Index Fund, and 15% to each of the Spartan Extended Market Index Fund, Spartan International Index Fund and Fidelity U.S. Bond Index Fund. Vanguard also has a fund of funds product line, Life-Strategy Funds, which invest in Vanguard index funds in different proportions, ranging from the most conservative (Income Portfolio and Conservative Growth) to the more aggressive (Moderate Growth and Growth Portfolio).

As is obvious from these examples, U.S. investors enjoy a cornucopia of choice in their index strategies that Canadians can only envy. But while domestic investors are still the poor cousins, Canadians can nonetheless use these index principles at the very least in managing the U.S. component of their portfolios and they apply equally to managing Canadian holdings. Again, as the S&P/TSE family matures, with small- and mid-cap product development almost certainly on the way to complement the new crop of big-cap S&P/TSE 60 funds and other index products that are coming, Canadian indexers may soon have the same diversification edge that their U.S. counterparts currently enjoy.

Guidelines from Schwab Research

In a recent study, leading U.S. discount broker Charles Schwab undertook extensive research that points to the fact that employing indexing as the core for a long-term U.S. equity portfolio will produce optimal results. In doing so, the Schwab researchers tried to quantify by asset class what proportion of funds should be committed to index funds and actively managed funds based on certain sector or market cap allocations. Key research findings include the following not un-expected results:

- The use of index products as core portfolio holdings lowers over-all portfolio risk.
- Partial use of indexes actually improves the chance of beating the index return.
- Actively managed funds are best used in conjunction with core U.S. index funds for international and small-cap markets.

In its research, Schwab compared a wide sample of actively man-aged fund portfolios, an equal number of portfolios with a combina-tion of index and active funds, and an all-index portfolio. The screening process was specifically designed to identify the optimal combination of index and actively managed funds with the highest probability of simultaneously outperforming the market by the largest amount, while underperforming the market by the smallest amount (aka the best of all possible worlds). The index proxies were the S&P 500, the Russell 2000 for small-caps and the MSCI EAFE as the international bench-mark (note this is ex-Japan, which is a double-edged sword given the recent resurgence of that equity market).

The key results of the study indicate that:

- Investors wanting exposure to large-cap U.S. stocks should allo-cate 80% of their portfolios to the index funds that track this por-tion of the market (typically the S&P 500 but also other index funds) and only 20% to actively managed funds.

- For small-cap stocks, the study recommended that only 40% go into small-cap index funds and 60% into actively managed funds.
- For international exposure, the index portion should be 30%, with 70% committed to active management.

These findings are not intended to be hard-and-fast rules, and the Schwab study stresses that the percentages cited are guidelines, not mandates. There are also obviously different investor comfort levels that are at the heart of the active/passive investment divide. Nonetheless, the Schwab findings provide a good jumping-off point as to where investors may wish to begin their core and explore strategy, with approximate proportions for index products as the core and managed funds as the explore if anyone thinks he/she is going to be able to outperform the market. Ironically, but not unexpectedly, the study provides no pointers as to how to pick managers who can outperform. So we're back to square one again.

Have We Missed Anything?—Myths about Index Investing

This will be the end of the road for most index investors, so before exploring more aggressive index strategies which are clearly only appropriate for index traders (pp. 190 ff.), perhaps we should take stock of anything we may have missed in the discussion thus far. The best way to conclude may therefore be to consider what index investing is not:

1. Index investing is not just about one index, and one index, such as the S&P 500, isn't really the market although it is a market, and an important one. An S&P 500 mutual fund is simply a fund that's indexed to the S&P 500.
2. Index investing is not a no-risk investment option. It's low cost, low turnover and tax efficient, but any index fund is just as risky

as that portion of the market it is trying to track—no more, no less. There is always market risk, and index funds respond as the market goes up, down and sideways. Index investing is also not a guarantee of not losing money in any given year or number of years.

3. Index investing is really only intended for some types of equities (i.e. big-cap names). Not so. Indexing has proved to be very effective in many areas of the market, from small-cap stocks to the broadest measures of market performance. And, of course, indexing isn't just restricted to the stock market. It can be used effectively in the bond market (see *Gentlemen Prefer Bonds*, pp. 144 ff.) and for many other types of financial asset.

4. Index investing always outperforms. In fact, indexing per se neither underperforms nor overperforms. All that you can say is that an index product performs as well as or worse than or better relative to the broad universe of active fund managers tracking the same benchmark. Incidentally, when an index such as the S&P 500 is outperforming in that sense, indexing gets a good name (in the case of Canada, it would be, if the TSE 300 *were* to outperform, indexing *would* have a good name, etc.) When it is underperforming, it gets a bad name. This is called blaming the messenger syndrome (see p. 47).

5. The S&P 500 will always outperform 80% of active fund managers in any given year. This is more of the same. While it may be true that almost 80% of active managers don't consistently beat the bogey, the inverse is not true. Nonetheless, an index fund is susceptible only to market risk. Actively managed funds, on the other hand, contain two components of risk: market risk and manager risk—the odds that the fund manager may get it wrong and consequently underperform.

6. Index funds can get too big for their britches (i.e. in assets) and cease to be effective investment vehicles any longer. While it's true that rock star investor interest in index funds can have a snowball effect, the liquidity of index stocks is such that it is always possible to invest new fund assets or purchase new index names— but obviously, at a price. If anything, it is active funds that suffer from becoming too large.

7. Even if index investing does have all the benefits that have been attributed to it, it still makes a significant statistical bet of its own—and that is that the bogey is the market. Dear reader, if you believe that at this point, you have just wasted $24.95.

TACTICAL INDEX INVESTING:
THE HEDGED INDEX INVESTOR

The strategic or buy and hold index investor is like someone who has just purchased a house: he/she is committed for the longer term. The hedged index investor, on the other hand, isn't quite so sure and would rather have a short-term lease and then decide about buying later. Index derivatives are the enabling vehicles that permit an investor to "rent" the market rather than committing to a full down payment and mortgage obligation, but hedged investors can also use index derivatives as a means of ensuring different degrees of control over their portfolios. With index derivatives, investors still get all the index benefits, including convenient one-stop investment exposure, broad market diversification, etc., etc., but only for the limited amount of time the derivative contract is in force (see further index option pricing notes, pp. 120 ff). The chief use of index derivatives are for:

- Market participation strategies (both bull and bear) based on the investor's market view and timing constraints.
- Portfolio insurance or hedging strategies to protect an existing index portfolio against short-term market volatility.
- Arbitrage and other related trading strategies to attempt to exploit anomalies in current valuation levels.

Buy and hold investment strategies have worked pretty well for savvy folk like Messrs. Templeton and Buffett and they also work pretty well for index investors generally. While no one is suggesting that index fund investors should rush out and start trading index options, they do have a place in the overall index investing universe. Index derivatives and their related strategies, however, also raise the question of short- versus long-term investment thinking (see comments on day trading, p. 200). Investors are generally long term because their financial requirements are long term. But there is nothing morally superior about being a long-term investor; it's just that your odds of not losing money are greater and market timing on a very short-term basis is little more than a crap shoot. On the other hand, many professional investors have subscribed to the findings of academic research that indicate it is possible to increase portfolio returns significantly through forms of tactical asset allocation as opposed to simply maintaining a buy and hold strategy. Nonetheless, index derivatives permit the hedged index investor to worship at the temple of profitability, not necessarily consistency, by permitting degrees of market timing over various time horizons. After all, an investor with a 20-year time horizon is market timing in a sense, too; the question here is one of relativity, not absolute kind.

The advent of index derivatives has given investors more flexibility in implementing strategies based on their market view than was ever possible before. Beyond employing any of the cash market index products we have been considering, an investor who feels that the market will rise in the near future may now do one of three things: buy index call options (least risk), buy index futures (most risk) or buy a portfolio of individual index stock call options (in the smaller indexes, at least, options are traded for all index component stocks, which can give rise to some interesting arbitrage strategies, see below). Alternatively, if an investor believes the market may decline in the near future, the choices include selling futures, buying index puts or puts on individual index stocks. Obviously, trading in index derivatives turns the investor into a sort of amateur portfolio manager, a role that requires market sophistication in addition to a specialized brokerage account for options (and separate account for futures trading). In addition, index derivatives are to all intents and purposes disallowed in RSPs and the Canadian investment dealers take a fairly dim view of index option traders (at least on the short side), a situation which does not prevail to the same extent in the U.S., where index option and futures traders are important business, although the advent of SPDRs and other related, non-time restricted index vehicles are providing strong competition.

The primary U.S. index options are SPX, which tracks the mighty S&P 500, OEX for the smaller S&P 100 and NDX for the big-cap tech Nasdaq 100; in Canada, the most liquid contract has been TXO, which tracks the Toronto 35 Index. The future of all index derivatives in Canada is currently up in the air, pending among other things the realignment of the four Canadian exchanges into senior market, derivative market, venture capital market, etc.; the fate of the existing Toronto derivative family; and future product development around the S&P/TSE 60 Index.

Again, to view the totality of the index investing opportunity, we will consider some of the basic and most sensible index derivative strategies, including the use of index options and longer-term LEAPS. Both index calls and puts provide market exposure and an insurance element but over a restricted time horizon. In addition, the insurance benefit of buying puts can be replicated by shorting index products such as SPDRs and TIPS, but with a very different risk profile, since the maximum loss with a purchased option is the premium you have paid for it, while a short position of any kind puts the investor on the hook for any increase in the index level from whence the short was declared until it is covered. Investors can also use index participation units (say SPDRs) and their corresponding index options (in this case SPX) to create some interesting positions (example: use an SPX covered call option writing strategy to hedge an existing SPDRs position—i.e. your synthetic S&P 500 portfolio—against market volatility). In all these strategies, transaction (brokerage) costs can have a substantial effect on return on investment and should be factored into the investor's P&L. For notes on index futures, see below.

Index options use a multiplier just like stock options but with one important difference: the multiplier represents $100 instead of 100 shares of stock. To calculate the dollar value of an index options contract, the index level is simply multiplied by $100. For example, an OEX index level of 650 × US$100 equals an underlying dollar value equivalent of US$65,000 per contract (i.e. this is the dollar amount of S&P 100 stock you control with the contract). Similarly, an option premium quoted at US$16.50 represents US$1,650 ($16.50 × $100) per option contract. As the major indexes have raced towards the sky in recent years, the cost of buying options has increased accordingly, placing them outside the reach of the small speculator, perhaps a good thing.

Index options also come in two forms. While most stock options are American style, which means they can be exercised at any time at the discretion of the holder prior to expiry, index options which are used to hedge portfolios are traditionally European style, i.e. they cannot be exercised until expiration. This can be a crucial consideration in employing some sophisticated index strategies (see synthetic futures, below). How this works in practice is that an institutional fund which owns the banks or tech stocks or whatever, instead of trying to hedge the individual stock positions by buying puts on each of them (which can be an expensive process), will buy index puts, which provide blanket index or sector coverage over the term of the insurance policy. This is an imprecise hedge but in the view of many managers better than nothing. Since institutions typically use puts to hedge long positions and retail investors tend to use calls to gain market exposure, professional traders monitor the comparative trading volume in each (termed the put/call ratio and calculated for both individual stock options as well as index options) to get a sense of market sentiment. This has largely replaced the old-fashioned odd lot indicator as a key market barometer (in both cases, the little guy is assumed not to know what he/she is doing).

So much for the essential details. The most important question in all of this is, are index options a waste of money? First of all, index option pricing essentially reflects volatility, which is an input, not an absolute, based on the future unpredictability of the underlying index share prices. Some traders evaluate option premium levels by their gut, some by sophisticated software packages which focus on fair value analysis, some by market or individual sector/equity fundamentals. But the key point about index option pricing is that you are obliged to pay what the market makers say the contract premium should be so it is an essentially academic question unless you have the capacity for sophisticated market analysis and the resources to arb out any cash market/index option pricing anomalies. The other point is that buying index options is generally considered a losing strategy because something like 60% of all contracts expire worthless. These are real considerations, but for the hedged index investor, the flexibility index options affords can outweigh these probability-related factors. Remember, an at-the-money option is telling you that you have a 50/50 chance of not losing money. But since part of the reason for buying index options in the first place is as a form of insurance (both long and short) for an investor's portfolio, the hedged index investor will pay up for the protection in the same way that one purchases auto or home insurance. Similarly, for option writers, the desired result of this strategy is to see the contract expire worthless. While there are a lot of ridiculous strategies out there, index options can be a useful adjunct for the index investor, so it is best to understand them in a general way even if you never put them to use in your portfolio.

Index Call Option Strategies

Investors generally purchase index calls because they are bullish on the prospects for the market as a whole. Besides providing a convenient and cost-effective way of implementing the investor's market view, index calls also offer significant leverage potential. Since investors frequently have different perceptions as to the future price movement of the market, index options are listed with expiration months ranging from the nearby month out several months. Index options are universally conceded to provide the investor with these benefits:

- Short-term equity index exposure with limited risk.
- The benefit of leverage.
- Portfolio diversification and risk reduction.

The most common applications for employing index call options are:

1. Index substitution. Index call options can be used as a short-term synthetic index portfolio. Investors may not wish to buy the various index stocks, index funds or index participation units outright at a certain time for a variety of reasons. Instead, they can purchase index call options and still achieve the indexing benefits of one-stop market exposure and portfolio diversification over the life of the contract.

2. Investment leverage. Index calls allow the investor to benefit from index price movement at a fraction of the cost required to purchase a dollar-equivalent value of index shares or many other index products outright. For investors who do not wish to use all of their capital to purchase the underlying index in whatever form, buying index call options provides a viable alternative with limited risk. The most an investor ever has at risk is the option premium paid. A simple method of participating in the price potential of the index, while also earning income, is to buy calls and invest the remaining funds in an income-bearing vehicle such as T-bills (the so-called 90/10 strategy).

3. Anticipatory hedge. Index call options can also be used as insurance against an anticipated rise in the price of the index stocks. By purchasing an index call, investors can establish the maximum price they are willing to pay for market exposure. If during the life of the option, the market value of the index declines below the exercise price, the investor may let the index call option expire worthless or sell the option to recover part of the premium.

Index Put Option Strategies

Index put option strategies are essentially the mirror image of index calls. Investors generally purchase index puts because they are bearish on the prospects for the market as a whole. Besides providing a convenient and cost-effective way of implementing the investor's market view, index puts also offer significant leverage potential.

Again, the key benefits of employing index puts include:

- A leveraged way of participating in the downside of a market index with limited risk.
- An alternative to short-selling the index.
- Market or portfolio insurance.

The most common applications for index put options are:

1. Leverage with limited risk. Index put buyers believe that the market will decline and want to do something about it. Just as index call buyers can enjoy greater leverage than stock buyers, index put holders have greater leverage potential than short-sellers. Short-selling is the sale of an underlying interest which an investor does not own. This is a strategy suitable only for sophisticated investors. The advent of put options has virtually obviated the need for short-selling for index products or other optionable securities (i.e. individual stocks).
2. Portfolio insurance. Regardless of current market volatility, most investors do not tend to sell all of their holdings even when index prices are expected to decline. An alternative to selling all or part of an index portfolio is to buy index puts as insurance. As illustrated in the previous example, put holders generally profit as the price of the underlying security declines. Therefore investors can offset part or all of the unrealized losses on their index positions by purchasing puts prior to a market decline. As with index calls, index put option buyers pay the contract premium and have no further financial obligation.

General Considerations for Buying Index Options

Despite their market participation and insurance features, all index options provide more of a trading rather than an investing perspective on indexing. That's why they're certainly not for everybody:

- Never employ more than 10% of your total investable funds for buying index options.
- Generally, options which exhibit high implied volatilities offer the best opportunities for profit because the implied volatility is telling you to expect a big move; on the other hand, this same factor means that you are also paying up for the privilege. Index options are, however, generally less volatile than individual stock options.
- Buy options with sufficient time remaining to expiry to ensure you benefit from any indicated index price movement. Trading the nearby month is a day at the track.
- Take your profits, don't let them run. Index options are a wasting asset with the greatest decay of time value occurring during the last weeks to expiration.
- Cut your losses. If the index is not moving, either cut your losses or roll-out in time (i.e., sell the existing index contract and buy an option with a longer maturity).

The Advantages of Index LEAPS

Long-term Equity AnticiPation Securities (LEAPS) enable investors to benefit from long-term, warrant-like exposure to a range of U.S. indexes, including the Dow, S&P 100 or OEX and the S&P 500. (LEAPS index products are listed on the CBOE.) To recap, like shorter-term index options, index LEAPS give the owner the right to purchase or sell the index at a specified price on or before a given date up to two years in the future. Unlike index options, but like warrants, index

LEAPS have a longer life span which makes them more attractive than short-term option products that suffer from time decay. In addition, since warrants are not available for the major U.S. indexes, LEAPS provide investors with a warrant-like alternative to index options.

While index LEAPS are very similar to index options, they do have several important differences:

1. Index LEAPS provide cost-effective portfolio diversification over a mid-term investment time horizon. Because LEAPS cost less than their respective underlying index stocks, the cash outlay for purchasing a LEAPS contract will be lower than purchasing index shares outright, providing some investors with greater diversification than they might otherwise be able to afford over the life of the contract.

2. Index LEAPS can also be used for leverage. By buying LEAPS index options, investors can utilize the inherent leverage of long-dated options to maximize returns.

3. Index LEAPS can be a useful hedging instrument. Investors concerned about downside market movement can purchase LEAPS puts to reduce the risk of loss. LEAPS offer a hedging capability of up to two years, more than twice the longest expiry of current exchange-listed equity index options.

4. Since index LEAPS have a greater time horizon than index options, the time decay experienced by LEAPS is initially not as rapid as is the case with short-term index options.

DYNAMIC INDEX INVESTING: THE INDEX TRADER

Just as this book was going to press, the North American media was full of the horrific killings at two Atlanta, Georgia brokerage offices by a day trader who had racked up over $100,000 in trading losses. If the point of investing is to create security, particularly for one's family, this incident simply reflects obscenity. But technology, the rise of the self-employed trader and leverage—that is margin provided by investment dealers—have contributed to the rise of the day trader and the attendant casino approach to managing assets that is all too evident today.

The advent of day traders and index day traders is not new, but it is a phenomenon that is clearly on the rise. In fact, futures traders were the original day traders, although of course it has always been possible (though not necessarily profitable because of high commissions and large bid/ask spreads) to trade stocks on a minute-by-minute basis during the hours the market is open. But this time it may be different. Equity trading via the Internet is booming and threatening to challenge the dominance of the traditional full-service brokerage houses (although they are actively trying to do something about it. Even Goldman Sachs and Merrill Lynch are getting into web stockbroking). Today, it is estimated that nearly 15% of all stock trades in the U.S. take place over the Internet and that number is growing daily. Clearly, a substantial amount of day trading assets is being diverted away from mutual funds or at least from what would otherwise have been committed to active or passive funds (fund flows have been slowing conspicuously in both the U.S. and Canada in the first months of 1999). What's more, day traders playing tech and other stocks have had a very good run for their money, and the Internet IPOs and individual issues themselves have been among the most highly profitable areas of the market to be in, although one often avoided by most professional fund managers.

What is curious about this investor "success" story is the fact that many day traders don't even know what the stocks they are investing in. Stocks? They're just a bunch of ticker symbols to be bought and sold at the click of a mouse. As the curious, naïve and/or greedy junior Gordon Gekkos sign up for their two-week training courses and plunk down their $50K of investable assets, some will stay but most will go. But in addition to the risk of not knowing what you are doing, or picking the wrong stock or getting out at the wrong second, there are other risks associated with the day trading phenomenon that have been recognized by the U.S. brokerage industry as well as by the SEC.

With some day trading firms, there has been excessive leverage, beyond the normal 50% margin accommodation provided by most brokerages, offered to investors; in many cases, day traders can arrange for funds from other third-party lenders and lever their accounts up as high as they think they can manage. To add insult to injury, now it's not just day trading. It is soon to become night trading. In response to proposals by the major U.S. exchanges to increase hours of operation, several major brokerages have taken steps in the direction of providing extended trading at least into the early evening hours. Off-exchange hours trading has existed for years via Instinet, the electronic order matching book run by Reuters which is now only available to institutional investors (why do these people still want to trade when they could go home? Often professional fund managers need to react to late-breaking news—typically earnings reports out just after the close, a press release about the firing of a CEO or merger or acquisitions activity—and need a conduit to make their investment decisions accordingly). The problem with these after-hours markets is liquidity. In the absence of much trading volume, bid/ask spreads can widen from cents to dollars and stocks bounce around so much that there can be major percentage movements from one trade to the next (this is truly market volatility). The only way to counteract rapid price changes in after-hours markets is to use limit orders, which set a buy threshold if a the stock price drops. A limit sell order does the same job when you're selling. The main disadvantage of any limit order is that, unlike a market order, your trade isn't guaranteed to take place. But this is a digression.

Ironically, critics of modern day trading are repeating arguments virtually verbatim from the time the U.S. futures industry began to attract more than casual interest from individual investors during the 1970s. So in light of all of the foregoing and as we commence a very brief look at index futures to complete our examination of index investing, can any of this activity be described as prudent? The best one can say is that all investing is ultimately a matter of probability (i.e. positioning your portfolio against the "odds" offered by the marketplace) regardless of the investor's time horizon. Templeton and Buffett make long-term calls; professional traders and the growing legions of day traders make very short-term, second-by-second calls. It remains a paradox, but both short- and long-term strategies can be executed exceptionally poorly or exceptionally well; in any case, they both exist and are essential to the "speculator/hedger" dynamic of the capital markets.

Index Futures Trading

Since so much has been made of professional, Wall Street index trading (see Chapter 4) and its positive impact on the rise of index products for the retail investor and on market liquidity generally, we'll make some superficial comments about the structure of index futures trading, but without believing for a moment that any reader will likely be tempted to do so. If anyone is interested further, there is any number of good books on index derivatives readily available. Surprisingly, though, trading index futures can be simpler than trading equities. But to trade them, you need substantial cash reserves in the form of good faith margin (your initial stake), variation margin (the money you must pay or receive from the clearing corporation if your futures trades go against or work in favour of your position) and time as either an independent floor trader (a dying breed in Canada) or day trader using discount brokers or the Web as we have seen. The most important thing to remember about a futures contract is that its underlying value rises and falls based on what traders are willing to pay for it from moment to moment during the trading day, not just on the current market index level, because the contract's terms are settled months into the future.

The U.S. index futures contracts in the index trader's arsenal are the usual suspects: the Dow 30, the S&P 500 and the pint-sized mini S&P (with a multiplier of only $50, it's been designed for speculators), along with the S&P MidCap 400, Nasdaq 100 and the Russell 2000. In the U.S., discount futures brokers will provide execution of the leading index futures contracts on a share-equivalent basis for fractions of a penny per share. Investors are also not restricted to trading the domestic market. We have already considered the range of international products available to Canadian investors, but for the do-it-yourself index futures and options trader, there is a wide range of international index derivative products available as well. Some, like the Japanese Nikkei 225 index future, trade in Chicago at the CME. Other leading global index futures track the French CAC 40, the German DAX 30, the U.K. FTSE 100 and Dow Jones STOXX Index and trade in their respective home markets, although many North American futures brokers through their correspondent networks can execute on behalf of their domestic clients.

The most compelling feature of index futures—and of futures contracts in general—is their leverage potential provided by the contract margin requirements. An investor is able to benefit from a favourable change in the value of a futures position with a margin deposit that is equal to only a fraction of the contract's actual value (usually 10%). However, the leverage potential implicit in futures trading can also result in substantial losses if the market moves in the opposite direction.

As a result, trading futures is recommended only for sophisticated investors who are well capitalized and fundamentally understand market risk and leverage.

A traditional commodity futures contract is a standardized obligation to purchase (long) or sell (short) a specific quantity of a particular commodity during a specified delivery period. In the old days, the buyer of a futures contract held until expiry was obligated to accept actual physical delivery of the underlying commodity during the designated delivery period. Equally the seller was committed to make delivery during the delivery period. However, many buyers and sellers would frequently liquidate their positions prior to the commencement of the delivery period, which made delivery an infrequent occurrence. To liquidate open positions, buyers would simply sell their contracts and sellers cover or buy them back. In the case of most major global index futures contracts, no actual physical delivery of stocks takes place since the contract is settled in cash just like index options.

Participants in the futures market can be divided into two broad groups, hedgers and speculators, and both are essential components of a liquid market. Generally, hedgers are institutional investors, portfolio managers or corporations whose business in this case is index stocks, the actual underlying commodity, and buy or sell futures to protect their interest in the cash market. While a charged word, speculator simply means an individual who has a market view. Speculators are individuals who possess risk capital which they use to buy and sell contracts to make a profit. In other words, hedgers use the futures market to minimize risk, which they in effect transfer to those who are willing to assume it, namely speculators.

Of central importance, all futures market participants have the flexibility to be long or short or a combination of the two depending on their market forecast. Futures trading strategies resemble other derivative strategies in terms of permitting investors to implement a long or short market view or hedging their portfolios. Remember, however, that futures trading differs markedly from other derivatives in terms of pricing and leverage potential (see pp. 116 ff.).

When index futures were introduced in 1982, they essentially commoditized the equity market (i.e. what's the difference between buying or selling index stocks as opposed to pork bellies or gold?). Index futures also helped highlight the usefulness of benchmarking to indexes and employing indexes as asset class proxies. Today, index futures are widely used to buy the market, sell the market and hedge the market by major pension funds and other institutional market players. In a sense, their development stands at the heart of what has become the index investing revolution.

Writing Index Call Options

Writing index calls is a widely used option strategy by pro traders and individual investors alike, but it is also risky in the same way that trading index futures is risky. Essentially, writing index calls exposes the investor to unlimited upside risk with nothing but the index premium as compensation. Nonetheless, and while this strategy is discouraged by many investment dealers, the main benefits of index call writing are the ability to:

- Earn incremental premium income.
- Hedge a portfolio against any decline in market value and/or to lower the adjusted cost base of the portfolio.
- Capture index volatility.

The two most common applications involving writing index call options are:

1. Incremental income and price protection. An investor who writes index calls against an existing portfolio is known as a "covered writer" since he/she owns the underlying index stocks. In return for writing the index calls, the investor receives premium income, but also assumes an obligation to sell the index at the exercise price if assigned. A "naked" writer is an investor who does not own the underlying index stock and may have to settle in cash if assigned, hence assuming a much riskier liability position.

2. Index volatility capture. We have seen that high levels of market volatility will significantly increases premium levels for equity index options. In this case, option premium levels will exceed fair value or the implied volatility of the contract will exceed the historical volatility of the underlying index stocks. Sophisticated investors or pro traders will write covered or naked index calls if they believe that the current contract premium level exceeds fair value. This is basically a volatility capture program. The principal focus of this strategy is to benefit from time decay as the index option pricing retreats to more normal levels and the investor can subsequently close out the position at a profit.

Writing index options gives rise to two further interesting strategies: synthetic futures and index/stock option arbitrage. Synthetic futures involve creating index futures positions out of index options. We have said nothing so far about writing index puts, but this is the mirror image strategy of writing calls with the same risk profile on the downside. A synthetic short futures position is long index put and short index call; a synthetic long position is long index call and short index put. With at-the-money puts and calls, it can be possible to create a virtually cost-free synthetic futures position, but the trick with these things is to make sure you're using European-style index options to avert early exercise. On this basis, synthetic futures can serve to hedge an index portfolio or as part of an index participation strategy. Obviously, the investor benefits only if the long position works out. Otherwise, your potential gain is limited to the option premium you take in and you are at risk to the extent that your call or put positions go deep into the money.

Another arbitrage strategy is to spread less volatile index options (i.e. go long the index to hedge the individual stock positions) against more volatile individual stock options (i.e. go short the individual stock options for premium capture). On a smaller index, a full basket of short stock calls against a long index hedge can produce interesting results if the implied volatilities of the individual stock options are running high.

THE INDEX DERIVATIVE CONTRIBUTION

It is instructive to compare the investment world before and after the introduction of equity index derivatives. I think it is fair to say that, given their flexibility, ease of use and multidimensional nature, index derivatives have revolutionized the way investors can manage their portfolios today:

Portfolio Objective:
A. Market participation
B. Hedging to control market volatility
C. Return enhancement

Before Derivatives:
A. Buy/sell stocks

B. Sell stocks
C. Not previously possible

With Derivatives:
A. Buy index call options
   Buy index futures
   Sell index put options
   Hold cash and index futures
B. Sell index call options
   Sell index futures
   Buy index put options
C. Write index call and put options
   Index arbitrage

Postscript

AS WE WENT TO PRESS, this item appeared on CNNfn (to whom thanks for authorizing permission to reproduce this article). As you can see, the index investing debate continues.

BATTLE OF THE $100B FUNDS VANGUARD'S 500 INDEX FUND SET TO CATCH UP TO FIDELITY MAGELLAN FUND

By Staff Writer Martine Costello
July 20, 1999: 11:25 a.m. ET

NEW YORK (CNNfn) - Fidelity Investments' flagship Magellan Fund passed a milestone recently when its assets topped $100 billion, but another mutual fund is poised to push it off its throne as the giant of the industry.

Vanguard 500 Index Fund is closing in on $93 billion in assets and could pass Magellan within the next few months as the nation's largest mutual fund, market watchers said.

"It's a healthy sign of the industry," said Russ Kinnel, an analyst at fund-tracker Morningstar. "You see the average investor is being treated well by the industry."

Besides size, the two funds could not be more different.

Magellan's returns have soared under the direction of famed stock picker Robert Stansky since he took the helm in 1996 amid suffering returns. Many analysts said his success helped chip away at the argument that size always hurts an actively managed fund. It has reigned as the largest mutual fund throughout the decade, analysts said.

Magellan owns both growth and value stocks, with top holdings as of June 30 in General Electric (GE), Microsoft (MSFT) and Home Depot (HD). It closed to most new investors in September 1997. The fund is up 16.67 percent year to date as of Monday, Morningstar said. Assets as of Monday were roughly $100.1 billion, Fidelity said.

"When we closed (Magellan), we were aware of the fact that it was likely some day another fund would surpass it, but that wasn't a concern of ours," said Fidelity spokeswoman Anne Crowley. "Growth in and of itself has never been our goal."

The Vanguard fund, managed by Gus Sauter, mirrors the S&P 500, owning comparable weightings of Microsoft, GE, IBM (IBM), Wal-Mart (WMT) and all the other companies in the index. The fund, with $92.64 billion in assets, is up 15.25 percent year to date as of Monday, Morningstar said.

"One-hundred billion is a big number but that's all it is," Sauter said. "I don't pay much attention to bragging rights. That's not what investors are concerned about. Investors are concerned with returns."

But what does it all mean for investors? Is big better or worse? Is indexing going to trounce actively-managed funds?

"You've got two low-cost, high performance funds," said Morningstar's Kinnel. "I would rather own a big fund than a tiny, no-name fund. Look at the resources behind Fidelity or Vanguard. You have a bunch of very talented people."

Magellan's passage of the $100 billion benchmark is noteworthy considering how poorly the fund was doing before Stansky took the helm from Jeffrey Vinik, Kinnel said.

"It means actively managed funds can adapt to big asset bases," Kinnel said. But at the same time, a big actively managed fund operates under restraints. For example, a big fund can't get in and out of positions very easily. So making unusual bets can backfire.

Kinnel recalled that Vinik in 1995 sold off some semiconductors and tech stocks and moved into bonds and large-cap value companies. His timing couldn't have been worse. When the market rebounded and growth stocks started to move, Vinik had to watch from the sidelines.

"You just can't jump back into the market with $15 billion when it rallies," Kinnel said.

One of Stansky's strategies has been to slide into a position as prices are falling. Last summer, when technology stocks were getting hammered, Stansky went shopping and returns soared.

To Index or Not to Index?

But even though Wall Street pays attention to Magellan's moves, Kinnel said he's seen more interest on Morningstar's message boards about the Vanguard fund.

"There's constant discussion about the Vanguard Index 500 Fund," Kinnel said. "If you say, 'I want a great index fund,' you think of the Vanguard 500 Index Fund. If you say, 'I want a great actively-managed fund,' there are many different names."

Kinnel said the Vanguard fund can be a good core holding for an investor.

A key difference with an index fund is that size does not really make a difference, said Lou Stanasolovich, a certified financial planner at Legend Financial Advisors in Pittsburgh.

"As long as it follows the index, size isn't an issue," Stanasolovich said.

Stanasolovich said he prefers building a portfolio around actively managed funds, but he thinks Magellan is too large. He wouldn't recommend it even if the fund were open for new investors.

Bill Dougherty, an analyst at Boston fund researcher Kanon Bloch Carre, pointed out that indexing is still a relatively small phenomenon on Wall Street among retail investors.

While 40 percent of the "defined benefit" pension plans—the old-fashioned pension plans your parents had—are indexed, it's a small chunk on the retail side of mutual funds, Dougherty said.

"Everybody is saying it's a big deal," Dougherty said of Vanguard 500 Index Fund hitting $100 billion. "But it's not. (Indexing) is not a saturated market. There's a lot of room for growth."

A good deal of that $90-plus billion in the Vanguard fund is from asset growth thanks to the meteoric rise of the S&P 500, Dougherty said.

And while indexing is growing more popular, there are signs that active managers are starting to win against the S&P 500 again, Dougherty said.

In 1993, 65 percent of active managers beat the S&P 500. The percentage started falling, and by 1997, only 10 percent of active managers beat the benchmark. But then things turned around. In 1998, 18 percent of active managers beat the benchmark, and in the second quarter of 1999 alone, 67 percent edged ahead of the index.

"Size as it relates to an index fund means nothing, but size as it relates to Magellan does mean something," Dougherty said. "The question is, is it all over for the index fund and do active managers have the edge? I don't know the answer to that."

Index